Uplevel Your Business,

Uplevel Your Life!

Four Pillars of

Successful Business Management

By: Kristen S. David

To my mother, you are the wind beneath my wings.

Table of Contents

Foreword

In law school, no one ever taught me how to run a successful business. While I started my first business in middle school, selling grape vine cuttings from my mother's vineyard, I didn't fully appreciate the enormity of balancing the pressures of being a business owner until I was a partner in a law firm. It was no longer just about the love of the legal field; all of a sudden there were so many things to juggle.

This book is a condensed version of all the little nuggets I picked up over the past twenty years about running successful businesses. My goal is to create the "entrepreneur's bible," so to speak, that I wish someone had put in my hands all those years ago. Goodness knows it would have saved many bad decisions, whether on a hiring basis to marketing and management decisions. Had I known these nuggets then, I would have gotten my life back and created a profitable business so much earlier.

I hope this book not only becomes a helpful resource for hundreds of experienced entrepreneurs looking to hone their skills, but also becomes the type of book that one reads and wants to give copies to their friends and other up-and-coming entrepreneurs.

Why reinvent the wheel when you could get the experience of those who have "been there, done that?"

Chapter 1: When Joy Turns to Juggling Turns to Chaos

It's 4:00 a.m. Your alarm hasn't even gone off, but you're wide awake, thinking of all the things you want to get done. If you could just get to the marketing piece, you can get more clients. If you could just get some time to work on that ad, maybe you could fire the employee who needs to go and hire someone who can really take some of this off your plate. If you can just get to...

The list goes on. You tackle the day with a plan that quickly flies out the window as one fire after another pops up, each one requiring resolution before you can move on. The day soon becomes a slippery slope, as you play firefighter to each new problem that arises.

You imagine the day when you are the fire captain and not the firefighter. You dream of owning a thriving, profitable business that is self-run with systems and a great team, but how do you get there?

There never seems to be enough time.

There never seems to be enough money.

You know you need great people to help do all the things that need to be done, but how can you pay someone else when you are barely paying yourself? Okay, let's be honest, when you are building your business, there are very often some months that are so tight you can't even take home a paycheck. You know you want to do more marketing to get more prospects, but again, you need money. It's like the chicken or the egg scenario – which one came first?

In your heart, you know your business could be amazing, but it is eating at you. It is costing you your sanity, your health, and your life.

Day in, day out, day in, day out, the grind just…never…seems….to…stop.

On the other side, you know there is a beautiful life with the ability to spend time with family and friends, and to take vacations and go back to loving your business. Heck, you see those social media pictures of successful business owners who are out fly fishing in the morning, relaxed and happy, and then post how they are excited to run a webinar that afternoon while their team runs the business.

How do they do it? The answer is this: SYSTEMS.

Chapter 2: I Was Once a Slave to My Business Too

I know how you feel; I had the same frustrations as my business ran my life.

For multiple years, I worked eighty-five-hour weeks, missing out on birthday parties, dinners, and social gatherings. Many nights, I worked until midnight or 1:00 a.m. If I did make it to a gathering, I was always late. My friends and family learned to accept it, and so did I.

In the early years, the finances sucked. My student loan payments were $1,500 a month and I was only making $2,000 a month. I didn't have enough take home money from work to pay all my bills, and on more than one occasion I had to use one credit card to pay another off. It sucked.

As a lawyer, I loved defending lawyers, doctors, dentists, chiropractors, and other medical professionals in malpractice actions. This gave me the chance to go into hundreds of offices and see what worked (and often what didn't work). I saw great teams that were hyper-productive due to established systems supported by a great culture. I also saw teams with qualified people who were not working together and instead created a lot of unnecessary chaos. I saw busy offices that were profitable. I also saw busy offices that should have been thriving and profitable but were not because there were no financial controls in place, let alone systems.

In my office, I learned to write a business plan and start growing my firm. I hired staff and fired staff until I finally honed the skill of finding and vetting great people as I built my "A-Team." Most importantly, I learned to focus my time and attention in balancing the different needs of the business. Part of that came from learning to build the systems that gave me my freedom. I learned to start documenting how I wanted things done and complete processes to ensure things were completed in a timely manner. I also taught my team to create, own and refine the systems in all parts of the business from the day-to-day management, the financials, and the workflows – everything.

After I doubled my business, re-wrote my business plan, and essentially doubled again, I was finally able to take true vacations. You know, an "off-grid," no contact, actually go and enjoy yourself vacation. These vacations were much different from the ones I took in the early years of my business, when I went on a five-day camping trip in the mountains and sat in the truck working on my laptop for the majority of the trip. I still remember sitting there, getting angry that there I was working and not enjoying my vacation, and yet I had no one to blame but myself.

Once I learned to balance my business, and it was running well with a solid team, I took one particular three-week long vacation, and the business did better when I was gone than when I was home. I will never forget returning to the office and when I started to ask lots of questions on how things were going my admin and assistant told me, "We know what we are doing, why don't you go on another vacation?"

At first, I was hurt that they didn't need me, but I quickly realized those might be the best words a business owner could ever hear!

Along this journey of growing my business, I was also given the opportunity to help other business owners build their businesses. Ultimately, I sold my business interests in my seven-figure law firm and focused primarily on helping business owners learn to run their businesses like a real business.

In the past fifteen years, I have worked with over 1,500 business owners. I have seen the inner workings of dentistry offices, orthopedic practices, chiropractic clinics, lawyers' offices, general businesses, and many, many others. I saw the struggles a business faces when it doesn't have the framework and systems for running profitably. I also saw the enormous joy and happiness of business owners who took the time to build the systems and, as a result, saw their profits increase, their business stabilize, and their personal income increase.

It is possible. There is life on the other side, and it's not just a pipe dream – it can be your reality. You can thrive in your life and your business.

Kristen S. David

Chapter 3: A Framework for Success

Business ownership can feel a lot like juggling – marketing, sales, hiring staff, managing staff, firing staff, hiring different staff, managing the services, trying to balance the financials, trying to keep everyone happy, and trying to take some money home at the end of the day.

Simply put, being a business owner is *exhausting* – until you learn how to juggle the many things you do by having sound systems and great people to help you. The first step is in recognizing the four pillars of a sustainable, profitable business.

Each chapter of this book could be an entire day-long course but what is inside is a condensed, quick read for every entrepreneur, so you glean the nuggets, sharpen your skills, and start building your business for success.

Pillar 1: Planning

For most entrepreneurs, the short-term goal is all about cash flow and creating some stability so you can breathe. Doing everything is exhausting, and yet there never seems to be enough time or money to do what you need to do. It is vital to create a game plan that will help you with that short-term need while also staying aware of the longer-term desire for profitability and more time. Finally, you must consider the end goal so that what you build is consistent with your far off, long-term goals. Do you wish to grow and scale? Or on the other hand, do you want to build to sell? Or both?

Pillar 2: Marketing/Selling

If you are not selling, then your business dies. It's that simple. The key to running a successful business is being clear on how much you need to sell to hit your goals and then building a marketing plan that works for those goals and to truly connect with the audience you want to connect with. The final step is to systemize the marketing, so it can run smoothly and continue to bring you the leads you need. This often entails building multiple marketing channels, so you have depth and do not get locked into only one pipeline of leads.

Pillar 3: Management

To run a successful business and free yourself from the daily grind, you generally need to hire people, but the question often is, "Who do you hire first?" The next question is, "Who do you hire next?" Using some objective tools, you can start to gain clarity on who you need and build a plan for surrounding yourself with a great team, both internally in your business, and externally, through vendors and outside consultants. Once you know who you want to hire, then it is about crafting a campaign to attract that ideal person who resonates with your vision and fits the culture you are building. However, it is not enough to only find great people; it is crucial to cultivate your employees, so they thrive, grow, and don't want to leave. However, sometimes we hire with great intentions, but it just turns out the hire is not the right fit. At that moment, it is essential to know when it is time to say goodbye and let that person go fly in a different environment. Finally, as an owner, you need to support your team and your business by ensuring they have the tools they need so the company can prosper.

Pillar 4: Financials

The bottom line is, *profitable owners are good money managers*! It's true. Profitable owners know their numbers; they know what money is coming in and where their hard-earned money is going out the door. It is important to use a variety of metrics to tell the objective story of what is going on in your company by using both lag metrics (metrics that tell you what has happened in the past, such as sales numbers, P&L, etc.), and lead metrics (marketing plan with hypothesis based on estimated conversion rates). Often financials can be intimidating, which is why it is so crucial to surround yourself with successful people to help you acclimate to that higher level of running your business.

So how do you balance all these "to-dos contained within the 4 Pillars?"

Running a successful business means balancing the competing needs and delegating tasks to people who can do them better than you. For most start-up businesses, in the beginning, those tasks all fall on the owner or a few, select individuals, but as the company grows, there are more opportunities to delegate to others. The most common problem is that no one taught us how to structure our focus on these competing needs, let alone how to hire great people.

There are 168 hours in every week – no more, no less. It is imperative to be intentional about your time and use it for the tasks that are best suited to the owner of a thriving business and learn to delegate down other tasks that are not the best use of your time.

These chapters will help you get clear on what you need to work on and how to plan out your growth in a way that doesn't kill you.

Pillar 1: Get Clear on What You Want

Kristen S. David

Chapter 4: Short Term Needs – Stability and Cash Flow

First and foremost, cash flow is king.

While you may have plans for the future, it is vital to assess where you are with cash flow right now and create a plan to build stability for your cash flow. In the beginning, you want to keep your 'hard-earned cash' close to the chest, and that means being cautious with how you spend your money to ensure that each dollar is being used in a way that will improve cash flow.

Building a Short-Term Plan

In the most basic sense, simply take an inventory of how much cash you will need for the next thirty days and compare that with the cash you have on hand and what money you expect to receive. This will help you identify the delta between the two for your immediate needs. You can then do that for three months and six months to see where you may fall short in the future.

If you want to build a stable business with less stress, this is the first exercise you need to do, so take a moment and do it right now and write down your answers to the following questions:

- Cash needed for the next 30 days (90 days, 180 days):
- Cash on hand:
- Cash expected:

- Subtotal cash expected over the next 30 days (90 days, 180 days):

- Delta between cash needed and cash expected:

Did you do it? Even if it is a sixty-second mental exercise, take the time to think about your answers. You will get more out of it if you do the full exercise, but if you feel you don't have time, just close your eyes and spend sixty seconds thinking about the cash you need.

Now you have a clearer picture of what you will need, and this is great. Now you have time to *make a plan* and ensure that you will bring in more than what is going out the door.

Pay Yourself First – Be Clear on the Mindset You Need for Profitable Success

For many businesses, there is not yet enough cash flow to support the needs of the company – or, frankly, there is just enough money to pay the expenses but not the owner. One of the most important things you need to do to be more profitable is to embrace the "profit-first mentality." In his book, *Profit First*, Mike Michalowicz sets out a straightforward methodology to get clear on the profit you want, subtract it from revenue, and then allocate the remainder of the funds for paying various expenses in a planned pattern. We will discuss this more in later chapters. For now, just roll with this idea.

This is a mindset shift for many entrepreneurs. Most of us grew up with the business concept that the owner gets whatever is left over after gross revenues less expenses. Unfortunately, all too often, there is little to no money left over for the owner, especially when the owner

14

wants to grow and plugs any extra money back into the growth of the business.

Short-Term Cash Flow Plan

If you want to run a stable, cash-flow positive business, then you need to do it with a plan. If you have additional expenses you wish to incur, great – find more people to help and get more revenue to cover it.

By now, you know whether or not you are on track for the short-term or if you have a delta. Now add in paying yourself. Are you still alright or is there a delta? If delta or tight, then let's make a plan to get you some money.

The quickest way to get money in the door is generally by reaching out to people who already know you, like you, and trust you, because getting money from strangers takes more time, as the audience needs to warm up to you.

For quick cash, think about who owes you money, who might want to buy from you again, or who might want to increase what they are getting. Next, you will look at who voiced interest in what you sell but didn't buy; follow up with that person. Finally, get out and network and talk to people about what you are doing and hustle up some business.

To better organize yourself and your pursuit for quick cash, jot down a "cash infusion plan," and answer these questions designed to help you find more money. After you do so, total the amount of money you have coming in.

- Money from people who owe you money (name the person and the amount)
- Money from people who might want to buy from you again
- Money from people who might want to increase their purchase
- Money from people who you think want to buy from you
- Money from new customers from hustling

Remember, cash flow is king! Make your plan and commit to following up with people and doing whatever it takes to bring in the cash you need. Don't wait – jump on this and get your short-term cash needs under control so you can breathe, so you can start planning the next stages, and so you can recognize that you are on the path to *thriving*.

Don't think. Just do. Pick up the phone and call people, send emails (although these are less effective because people get so many and it gets lost), send note cards (this is more effective if written with blue ink and a real stamp, because you will stand out from what the rest of the world does), or send a carrier pigeon (okay, highly unlikely, but definitely memorable). The point is, *do something*.

Chapter 4 Recap:

- Cash Flow is King
- Keep cash close to the chest

- Assess where you are and what you will need with the Cash Inventory Exercise
- Pay Yourself First! – mindset shift
- Build a short-term cash infusion plan

Finally, because this book is about reality and taking action, each chapter will end with action items to get you started.

Your Action Plan:

1. *Map out short-term cash needs*
2. *Map out short-term cash infusion plan*
3. *Start doing*

Kristen S. David

Chapter 5: Profitability and Peace of Mind…Is It Possible?

In growing a business, one of the most common misconceptions is that all your cash should be shoved back into growth. While it is true that it does take money to keep the company growing and building, it is possible to pay yourself a profit and use that profit to invest further in your business.

Every entrepreneur who has undertaken a business knows the feeling of questioning whether peace of mind could ever be a possibility. A company can start with such passion and quickly escalate into a storm of the unknown. Each day is filled with so many pressures and stressors; it is difficult to imagine a smooth-running business that is both well-managed and profitable. The great news is that it is possible!

However, "peace of mind" will be different for each business owner.

Imagine this: you, sitting on a beach in Hawaii. Your team is back at the office, where everything is running smoothly. The marketing systems are producing paying clients, your team is servicing those clients and creating raving fans, your financial controls ensure that there are checks and balances to the money coming in and the money going out, and the metrics illustrate that the company is doing well and projects growth over the next three quarters.

Yes, that can be possible! Re-read the above and picture yourself sitting on that beach.

Depending on the current situation in your business, it may take some time to create that life, but if you stay focused on what matters, you can get there. It takes time and energy to create clarity of how you want things done, but what is vital is to start documenting it so that everyone on your team has clear expectations of their job. As you proceed, you must also create the reporting mechanisms and a great culture (often driven by core values of productivity with KPIs (Key Performance Indicators)) to ensure everyone is operating at peak performance. Finally, you must systematize the business, the marketing, and the sales to ensure that the company has the right amount of business coming in.

The question becomes, are you willing to do the work necessary to create the solid foundation needed for this thriving, profitable, stable business? A business that can indeed operate without you there twenty-four/seven?

If you're reading this book, I suspect it is because you want to give it a try and get your business operating like as a real business should. So, let's get started on building a profitable business.

Profitability

People throw around the term "profitability" all the time, but not all uses of the word tell us the same story. So, let's head to the chalkboard and get clear on a few basic concepts that should have been taught in high school but likely weren't.

First, let's discuss *net profit margin*. The net profit margin tells us how much money remains at the end of the day. You can find this at the bottom of a profit and loss statement. *Gross profit margin* gives us clarity on whether or not the price of our product or service covers the cost of goods sold and still leaves us ample funds to pay for the operational activities and profit. You can calculate this by taking your total revenue less costs of goods sold and divide by the total revenue. If your gross profit margins are not where they should be, this will give you clear indicators that you need to be more efficient in your production or find alternative ways to reduce cost. Bottom line, if your gross profit margin is not adequate, you will have a challenging time increasing your net profit margin.

To be clear, anyone *can be* profitable. What stops most people is that it can be uncomfortable to price and sell sufficient quantities to ensure that revenue exceeds all expenses and still leaves profit at the end of the day. However, if you want it badly enough, if you're willing to do what it takes, and not settle, but keep at it until you hit your real goal, *profitability can be reached*. All too often, however, business owners get excited with the prospect of having others do the work for them and give away their profit and find themselves broke at the end of the month. For instance, purchasing expensive marketing with the hope that it is the magic pill before it is clear the business is ready for that marketing and that the investment can be supported by the revenues.

This is why it is essential to remain in the mindset, "If there's something I want, I need to go help more people and those additional product or service sales will fund that next step or desired expense."

So, let's dive into how to build a 10,000-foot view of your business strategy so it will be profitable. (A 10,000-foot look is the 'big picture', which allows you to build out a 5,000-foot view plan that is more granular, which in turn will enable you to build out the 1,000-foot view of what needs to happen day-to-day in the trenches.)

Build a Plan and Let Others Hold You Accountable

Part of entrepreneurs' success is that they conceive an idea and then formulate a plan for what they can sell and provide to their client base which then generates the revenue to pay for their new idea. They then execute on that plan and create the income necessary, and they don't stop until they have met their goal. This is where the rubber meets the road. Many of us have thought of money-making ideas, but we stop short upon the first hurdles. This is the "stick with-it-ness" that entrepreneurs need to be successful.

So, here's a game plan to make sure you stick with it.

1. Get clear on your goals or intentions.
2. Share your plans with at least five other successful business owners you admire. When you share your ideas with others, it makes them more real and increases the accountability factor.
3. Start executing on your plan.

4. When things get difficult, think of going back to those you told in step two and telling them that you didn't meet your goal. This will give you some additional drive to get out there and hustle and make it happen.

As entrepreneurs, we start the journey a bit green and ambitious but not clear on the extent of our full potential. Surrounding yourself with other successful individuals and coaches ensures that you will not bullshit yourself with false assumptions and stories. This is where it helps to have someone to guide you and hold you accountable to push you out of your own way. Look around you. Who is there that will call bullshit on why you're not profitable? If you don't have anyone, you need to find a good coach or mentor to help you on your journey, an ass kicker who has already succeeded in business and who will hold you accountable.

Chapter 5 Recap:
- Misconception: all money must go back into growth
- What is your "peace of mind"
- Get clear on what matters and make a plan to work toward those priorities
- Profitability: understand your net profit margin and your gross profit margin
- Decide on the profit you want and be resilient to obtain it
- Build a plan and let others hold you accountable

- Identify a short list of who you'd like to have hold you accountable

Your Action Plan:

1. *Get clear on your goals or intentions*
2. *Share your plans with at least five other successful business owners you admire*
3. *Start executing on your plan*
4. *Have an accountability partner*

Chapter 6: Long Term – Grow and Scale or Build to Sell?

Unicorns – in the entrepreneur's world, they do exist. Some businesses have grown exceedingly well and have reached the pinnacle to an almost mythical stature. Think tech companies who exploded on the scene and got sold, or successfully sold their first public stock, for billions. While few owners will hit that "bases-loaded home run," so many more will hit home runs and build successful companies that someone else wants to purchase.

Ah, but aren't these just pipe dreams? No, they are not. If you are interested in the possible, eventual sale of your business, or equity shares in your business, building your business the right way will make it much more attractive to a potential buyer. In fact, your success may well attract buyers even when you were not looking for them. On the other hand, if you load up your businesses with lots of debt and garbage, and not many people want to touch your business.

So, you might be thinking, how do you start contemplating about the end when you aren't yet sure what you want to do three, five, or ten years from now? Well, the first step is to get clear on your options. Always remember set out to build an awesome business because then the long-term goals become self-fulfilling.

Grow and Scale

Once you work on stabilizing your business and have some rock-solid profit, the focus turns to how you grow and scale your business. We will discuss this more later, but for now, let's talk about a few of the essential areas that will help you achieve these goals.

One of the most critical foundational elements before you can grow and scale is to build the systems. This means documenting how you want things done through policies, procedures, templates, and examples. This way, everyone on the team knows how to keep doing things the way you want them done and the way they need to be done to streamline the process. In other words, what is needed to make the business last, flourish and grow.

The second principal component is having proper financial controls and reporting. This will allow you to know if your firm is going off the rails so you can step in and make changes before it does get off track.

The final component is to turn up the dial on your marketing. This sounds easy enough, right? Well, only when you have a clear roadmap to get you where you want to go.

Build to Sell

Think about what you would want in a business before you bought one. Would you want stability with a reliable team? What about policies and procedures to replace those good people if they leave? How about a distinct workflow, so there is clarity and consistency in the product or service your team handles? Would you look for concrete figures showing a history of six to eight quarters of profit? What about weekly and monthly reporting on the financials, key metrics, and KPIs on the firm. And finally, wouldn't you want to see a good marketing plan that shows how the business will continue to get the right clients?

You would absolutely look for all of these things, no matter what the product or service was that the business was selling.

A book I read multiple times as I was growing my business was *Built to Sell* by John Warrillow. Reading this was part of what helped me start to see my business from a different perspective. I considered what a prospective buyer of my business would want and how I could position the company's products and services to show potential buyers that it was a good deal. Warrillow points out that you want people to be confident in your business and your team, not in you. That means you need to build a company that services customers in a systematic, repeatable way.

The great news is that when you have this on your horizon, it is easy to build a strategy to get you to this end goal. Keep reading, to learn how to reach your goals and make your business appealing to a potential buyer of your company!!

Building a Plan to Get You to Where You Want to Go

Get clear on what you want, both in the short and long-term so you can create a business that gives you plenty of options to grow and thrive. Here are some examples of some goals you may wish to set for your company:

- Your business should be sustained by sound marketing systems, a clear sales process, great valued products/services, proper financial controls, and a team that feels valued, works happily and is fully vested in your business.

- Your business should aim for at least a fifteen-percent net profit margin and work to leverage technology and software to streamline tasks.

- Your business should build robust policies and procedures to help the team onboard new staff and train them on how to do a great job in their position. The team will also continue to build the policies and procedures to make them better every month, and your team will understand how they can improve so they can move up into other positions if they are interested.

- Your business should have strong financial controls, with both lead and lag metrics, to provide accurate projections and accountability to the goals.

Once you get clear on what you want, it is easier to map out quarterly milestones.

Tales from the Trenches

One of the reasons I was able to double the revenue in my business and then double again was by getting clear on what I wanted and then mapping out a plan. I first started with those overriding goals, which felt very similar to core values. I turned each statement into objective, measurable goals with deadlines. I then broke down each deadline into three to five interim steps or milestones to keep me on pace to my goals. I then assigned deadlines and calendared each one with a specific description, so I knew exactly what I needed to do and could answer yes/no on whether I hit the milestone or not. Taking the time to map this out is what made it so much easier to wake up each morning and actively build to a better future.

Chapter 6 Recap:

- Unicorns are rare, but successful businesses are being quite profitably sold everywhere – no matter what the price tag
- Grow and Scale: must build robust systems, have proper financial controls, then turn up the marketing.
- Build to Sell: Absolutely, build a business that services customers in a systematic, repeatable way.
- Build Your Plan: Get clear on what you want and craft a plan to get you there with sound systems, leverage technology, great people, solid product or service, worthy financial controls, and a rock-solid profit margin.

Your Action Plan:

1. *Get clear on your long-term goals (or at least ideas of what you might want) and map out elements like the above that would be your ideal outcome.*

2. *Map out quarterly milestones that will help position you get you where you want to go and set deadlines to those goals.*

3. *Start executing your plan.*

4. *Have at least one accountability partner.*

Pillar 2: Marketing/Selling

Kristen S. David

Chapter 7: If Your Business Is Not Selling, Then Your Business Dies...So How Much Do You Need?

Cash flow is king, and what makes cash flow is sales. Bottom line, no sales or transactions means no cash. The reality is that you can have the greatest systems and business, but if you are not making sales, or have a plan to make sales as part of a developing or changing product, then it all falls apart.

So, let's start at the base of sales. A sale is about helping people make an informed decision to move forward with you. "Sales" is an opportunity to help a person move from where they are toward a better place, where they want to be. At the heart of it, a sale is about helping someone else gain clarity about what they want and helping the person get clear on how you can help them move forward and achieve their goals.

Keep in mind, sometimes the client knows their problem, and sometimes your job is to help your customer see that you have a solution to a problem they didn't yet realize they have.

Story Time

In a dentist's office, a person comes in with a chipped tooth. After evaluation, the dentist outlines an entire treatment plan to not just resolve the issue with the chipped tooth, but to also handle cavities, cleaning, whitening, and other needs so the person can proactively take steps to have a great smile and healthy teeth.

In a chiropractic office, a person comes in with a particular back pain. After evaluation, the chiropractor recommends not just the immediate adjustment, but also regular treatments of massage to release the muscles and adjustments to get the spine back into alignment. The person will sign up for this because they want the long-term resolution, not just a quick fix to a reoccurring problem. The key is helping the patient understand that the short-term fix is not the answer they seek.

As you can gauge from these examples, sales are about an equal exchange. The person has to want what you have to offer, and you have to want to exchange cash for the product or service you are offering. The model goes like this: a potential client, with a problem, visits a business owner, who has a solution. The potential client has money to give to get the business owner's product or service. In exchange, the business owner gives their time, and the client receives the product or service.

Keys to Sales Mastery

A vital component of sales is to quiet the voices in your head and stay focused on the client/patient/customer. Business owners often kill a deal by stopping short of asking for the sale or worse, not asking for the right price. As a business owner, you need to know how much it costs to fully and profitability provide the person with what they need. Don't shortchange the customer by quoting a lower price that won't cover all the work you need to do.

Tales from the Trenches

I remember when I made my first $10,000 sale. A plumber came to me on a personal project that was in litigation. I would be the third attorney on the case and there was a lot of work that needed to be done to get up to speed before I could even commence drafting the petition that would need to be submitted. I remember sitting in our conference room thinking, *this plumber doesn't likely have the money to take on this project fully*. At that moment, I stopped myself and told the little neighbors in my head (i.e. my subconscious) to shush and stayed focused on the client and what would be needed to move him forward. I explained that I would need a $10,000 retainer to get started and that I would likely run through that in the first two weeks and that he would need to replenish with another $10,000 so we could proceed into litigation. Before I could blink, the plumber pulled out a checkbook and started writing me the two checks. This experience taught me not to listen to the little voices in my head that try to play on my self-doubts.

An Unwavering Belief in What You are Selling

Another vital element is the unwavering belief in the service or product. You have to believe in what you are selling – in your mind and your heart. You must believe it is a solution – the best solution – to a customer's problem. You must operate as an evangelist to some extent. Having the confidence, with every fiber that you have, that your offering/service is the right thing for your customer, that will drive the sale.

If you don't believe, you are not going to be the number one salesperson. You must have unwavering faith in the product, in the company, and in the company's ability to deliver the product (or service) and support the customer for as long as is needed (weeks, months, years, decades – this depends on the product or service). If you are a potential customer for your own product or service, you'd better actually be a customer since it is the most obvious demonstration that you are a believer and that you are personally vested in making use of your product or service.

No marketing can ever substitute that power of belief. The job of marketing is to deliver qualified leads. The job of sales is to convert those leads using collateral materials, testimonials, demonstrations, and, above all, belief and conviction.

That belief means that you also believe that what you present is the best for the customer. At a personal level, you know you are right for the customer; you want the customer to trust you and form a partnership with you in the transaction. That's high-class selling – solution selling. That's answering the needs of customers, whether those are conscious or unconscious needs.

If you can set up that partnership, it will take you one step further into marketing. When you have helped a customer succeed beyond their wildest expectations, they will become an evangelist for you. They will tell their friends, business associates, and other acquaintances. That's the multiplicative effect of "belief."

How Much Do You Need to Sell to Hit Your Goals?

The answer to this question depends on your average selling price (ASP), or the average value of your service or product.

For example, if you are a dentist whose goal is to hit $100,000 a month and your average client treatment package is $5,000, then you need to help twenty people.

If you are a counselor or a chiropractor and your average charges are $250, but after insurance you only get about $140, you have to service a lot more people. Say you want $30,000 a month – you would need to service 214 people. However, what if you could increase the average service to $170 by taking a mix of non-insurance patients and insurance patients; then you only need to see 176 patients in the month. With an average of twenty-two productive days in the office, that's only eight patients a day.

Conversion Rates

Once you are clear on how many people you need to help, you must get clear on how many leads need to come in the door to convert enough people into paying clients to hit your goal. Leads are prospective clients. They might be hot leads (people ready to sign up immediately), warm leads (interested people) or cold leads (people who show interest at some point but are no longer as active in what you are doing).

It is essential to know your overall conversion rate. If you are not already tracking these numbers (which you must do), then simply think about the last ten potential clients who you had an honest conversation with about what you do, and you proposed they work with you. How many hired you or bought your product? Did three out of ten people buy your product or services? If so, that is a thirty percent conversion rate. That means if you want fifteen customers, you need to talk to approximately forty-five people. If your conversion rate was fifty percent, you would only need to talk to thirty prospects to get to fifteen customers. See, the higher the conversion rate, the less time and money you need to spend on marketing.

Conversion rates based on the source of the lead are another noteworthy component to conversion rates. For example, in many industries, we see the following conversion rates:

- Referrals from raving fans (acquaintance/former client): three out of four will hire you, a seventy-five percent conversion rate
- Referral from a professional referral source: two out of four will hire you, a fifty percent conversion rate
- Seminar, webinar, speaking event, community event: one out of four will hire you, a twenty-five percent conversion rate
- Online source (website/ad/online directory): one out of ten will hire you, a ten percent conversion rate

When laid out in black and white, it is easy to see that the lead who comes to you from people who know you, like you, and trust you (backend marketing) has been warmed by your acquaintances, former clients, referral sources, and are more likely to hire you. On the other hand, if the person comes from front end marketing, where they don't yet know you, like you, or trust you, (like online sources) the lead needs to be warmed to get to know you and is less likely to hire you initially.

Another consideration is whether the person is a "qualified lead" as opposed to just a random lead. A "qualified lead" means they are the right type of client for you. Once the person reaches out to you and you can confirm they are qualified, the person becomes a prospect.

Knowing your conversion rates by source, as well as your overall conversion rate places you in control of your numbers.

Increasing Your Conversion Rate

As you build out your business plan, you will want to make a plan to increase your conversion rate quarter by quarter and diversify your marketing, so you bring in leads from a variety of sources to even up your conversion rate.

Start with mapping out some quarterly goals with various training, education, and ways to hone your sales skills. For instance, in the first quarter, read two sales books, work with a coach, take an online training course on sales, and start tracking your sales metrics.

In the second quarter, review sales metrics and assess conversion rates by source and reasons why people don't hire you and work with a coach to sharpen your intake and sales process to use a structured framework for more consistency.

In the third quarter, focus on enhancing your skills on handling objections (excuses like having no money, no time, or the need to think about it).

Finally, in the fourth quarter, record sales conversations and then review the recording and break down where the sale fell apart and refine your skills based on your areas of need.

Building a plan that will help you grow and hone your skills is a vital part of successful business management and will help you stay aligned with your goals.

So How Many Sales Do You Need to Hit Your Goal

Back to the beginning. If your business is not selling, then your business dies, so how much money do you need?

First, start with your financial goals and divide this by your average value. For example, if you want to bring in $30,000 in revenue and the average value for your service is $1,500, your equation will look like this: ($30,000 goal/ $1,500 average value = 20 clients). This number gives you how many people you need to help or how many matters you need to service. In this example, the number is twenty.

The next step is to retrieve (or estimate) your overall conversion rate and apply it. If our overall conversion rate in this scenario was thirty percent, we would divide the number of people you need to help (twenty) by your conversion rate (0.30): (20 clients/.30 = 66 potential clients.). This gives you the clarity of the number of prospects you need to speak with. In this case, we would need to talk to sixty-six potential clients.

Setting up Sales Systems

As your business grows, it is imperative to create repeatable processes for your sales. Whether you are using technology or human interaction to help get sales, it is crucial to map out the process so it can be replicated.

Start with the overall process and then begin building in the scripts, the templates, and the materials to ensure that it is consistently being done the way you want. In this way, you can hire others to handle or oversee the sales process and be assured that it is being done the way you want.

The "Sales" Process can seem daunting to think about mapping out but, in reality, it just requires some pen to paper action. I have done this with dozens and dozens of business owners, and the biggest key is "Just Get Started". Whether on a poster sized post-it or the back of a napkin, start mapping out the customer journey. Box #1 might be when they initially contact your business. This might be by website chat, by telephone or by an actual purchase. Then draw an arrow and draw box #2 and note what that step entails. This might be that the potential client gets some information. Then draw an arrow and draw box #3. This might be a sales consultation where you gather information to determine the right product or service for the person. Continue drawing until you document the full customer journey.

Tales from the Trenches

In one of the four-day workshops I have run, one of the favorite exercises has been when we mapped out the intake and sales process through to the workflow process. Imagine two dozen law firm owners with large post-it's on the walls of a conference center with big colored markers mapping out the process. Each business (criminal law, family law, personal injury law, estate planning, etc.) has a slightly different process making each distinct, and yet they all have commonality. First Contact -> Initial Engagement -> Triage Potential Client -> Determine Best Option for Sale -> Convert to Paying Client -> Onboard Client.

As you start to write out your process, you will soon go from graphing the big picture sequence to adding in details of the client journey. This will help you see the overall system, and give you clearer insight on how to simplify the journey. This will allow you to refine your policies, procedures and systems for selling as well as help you improve the customer experience, so they feel well-taken care each step of the way.

Chapter 7 Recap:
- What makes cash flow is sales
- "Sales" is about helping people make an informed decision to move forward with you
- "Sales Mastery" is about quieting the voices in your head
- Understand your average selling price and your sales conversion rates

- Calculate how many sales you need
- Craft a plan to increase your conversion rates
- Create sales systems with a map of your client's journey

Your Action Plan:

1. *Calculate how many customers you need to help to hit your financial goals*

2. *With your conversion rate, calculate how many prospects you need to speak with to meet the revenue forecast in your plan*

3. *Map out a quarterly plan of how to improve your conversion rate*

4. *Craft a sales plan for how the business will continue to make sales without you, the owner, doing all the work by mapping the client journey, creating systems and hiring staff*

Kristen S. David

Chapter 8: Honing in on Your Ideal Client and Crafting a Marketing Plan That Gets You to Your Goals

What do you like to do and *who* do you want to work with as your typical customer?

There are a lot of people in this world you can help, and a lot of products or services that could be built. The key is finding things you like to do and working with the people you want to work with who will pay you profitably for what you are offering to them. Don't just sell anything and don't just work with everyone. Focus on what you like so you can do what you genuinely enjoy.

For instance, some doctors really like the consulting and planning versus purely performing procedures. Some chiropractors' specialty is recent car accident injuries versus long-term issues. Similarly, some architects like working with someone who already has ideas for a project while others like working with someone with a completely blank page and no expectations.

Now that you have decided who you want to work with, *what* are their problems?

If you haven't already done this key step in preparing your marketing, the time is now. Think about your ideal client and what the entire nature of their problem is. Too often we just focus on the immediate need and not the overall problem. You need to tap into their real concern and how you can help them move forward. Set a memo to yourself: always know and articulate the problem you are solving before you build the solution.

For example, when someone buys a drill and drill bits, is it because they want to buy a drill and drill bits or because they want to make holes? If you could sell them just the holes, your business would skyrocket. While you can't always sell the end goal, you can position your company to be the right company to help them move forward.

The bottom line is that it is easier to convert clients when you tap into what people truly want. This is called positioning, and you position your offerings to be the best solution for what your clients want.

Your Ideal Client

A key to successful business management is that you must *drive* your marketing and *choose* who specifically you wish to attract.

A first step to centering in on your ideal client is to identify your buyer personas, a rough profile of one segment of your market. Let's look at three different example marketing personas in terms of basic demographics.

First, we have Ned and Nelly, the newlyweds. This couple is between twenty-three and thirty-years-old, and they have zero to two children, aged between one and six. This family rents an apartment or a house and has one to two cars. Ned and Nelly both work and juggle daycare fees and debt from student loans.

Next, we have Mark and Mary, the middle years couple. They are between thirty and fifty-years-old and have two children, between the ages of eight and eighteen. Mark and Mary work, own their own home and have resolved their debt, but are focused on paying for their children's' college. They have been saving some of their income and are starting to use their (now) surplus income on their hobby interests and major vacations.

Finally, we have Paul and Paula, the professionals between forty-five and sixty-five years old. Their children are grown, and they own their home and likely a second vacation property. Perhaps Paul and Paula also have a boat, motorcycles, or other toys or items related to their hobbies. They have a robust retirement portfolio.

From there, you can flesh out even more. Start considering what these buyer personas are interested in, where they like to visit, what they like to do, what their online activities are, where they buy products, etc. You will also want to build out their pain points, challenges, frustrations, and fears. Finally, you want to consider their wants, goals, and aspirations. This all helps you better understand your audience and enables you to tailor your marketing so it resonates with what they will buy to solve their problems or further their desires.

Let's go over a marketing exercise to put this into practice. Think through a day in the life of your ideal client. Write out their demographics, their interests, their wants, and their desires. Then answer these questions: what does this person do all day? Who do they talk to? Who are their trusted advisors? Where do they live? What is their daily routine? What are their pain points? What are their concerns? What are their most pressing needs?

Marketing personas help you get more precise about the overall segments, so you can then target specific individuals.

Once you know your overall segments, you can then build out one or two marketing avatars. An avatar is a fictitious character that embodies the key attributes you are looking for. You give them a name and specific demographics and get so deep into their lives and habits that they are practically real. You interview clients and gather data and analytics about their spending habits.

Here are three examples where we took the overall persona and turned one person into our ideal avatar:

For example, we can dive deeper into Ned, the new parent. Ned is twenty-three-years-old, is married, and has one child, a six-month-old. Ned rents an apartment, has one car, and works a nine-to-five job. He stresses about getting to daycare to pick up his daughter as the budget is tight and can't afford the extra hours at daycare. He struggles to pay his student loans and save for a house. Because of this stress on money, he spends a lot of time online searching for the best deals.

In the next avatar, we have Mary, the middle school teacher. Mary is thirty-four-years-old, with two children, ages fourteen and sixteen. Mary is married, and she and her wife own their home. Mary works for a school district and thus gets set time off for summer break and other holidays. Her debt is resolved, but she focuses on saving for college for her kids. Mary buys what her family needs, but they don't splurge.

Finally, we have Paul, the psychiatrist for professionals. He is fifty-six-years-old, with grown children. Like Mary, Paul is married and owns his own home. However, Paul also has a lake house, a boat for fishing, and a robust retirement portfolio. He loves great food and excellent wines and will spend $150-200 on a bottle of good wine. Paul's large purchases are made after consulting consumer reports, ratings, and reviews.

These three avatars give you greater insight into their concerns, pain points and daily life. This helps you position your marketing to the audience. For instance, for Ned, we might do a marketing campaign using the words like "deal," "discount", and "bargain". In contrast, for Paul, we might launch a marketing campaign using terms like "top-rated", "#1 seller", and "widely acclaimed". Bottom-line, understanding your avatars or target consumer helps you pin-point marketing that sells.

Marketing Channels

In the last chapter, we touched on backend versus frontend marketing. There are many names for this in different industries, but it all boils down to marketing to people who know you, like you, and trust you (backend marketing) and marketing to people who don't yet know you, like you, or trust you (frontend marketing).

Often this is also referenced in terms of frontend marketing to new customers who don't yet know you versus selling or upselling additional products to current customers with whom you have a relationship through backend marketing.

Bob Burg, in his epic book, *Endless Referrals,* establishes the key business principle that, "All things being equal, people will do business with, and refer business to those people they know, like and trust."

So, in building a marketing plan, it is crucial to craft a plan to generate referrals from backend marketing while always casting the net wider to fresh new areas with frontend marketing. In this way, you build a marketing plan that ensures you never get trapped in having all your prospects come from one source – that is a recipe for disaster.

Tales from the Trenches

I once worked with a small law firm who prided themselves that 99% of their business came from online advertising. Things had been going great for several months, and they were growing quickly from all the online leads. However, for those that have done online advertising for any length of time, you know it can be fickle. What works one day doesn't work the next. We tried to warn the business owner that he needed to diversify and develop more backend marketing to all the great clients he had helped in the past, but he didn't listen. Unfortunately, several months later everything came crumbling down when the online leads dried up and the phone quit ringing. The revenues plummeted from over $85,000 a month to less than $30,000. There was hope that the trend would reverse itself, but in fact, the online leads didn't reach that peak again for over six months. That is the problem with online marketing, one day things are going great and with no notice the algorithms change, and it can all dry up. In the meantime, the business almost went upside down while we worked on developing the backend marketing. Lesson: Diversify out your marketing.

Cost of Acquisition

The other important aspect of balancing your backend marketing with your frontend marketing relates to the cost of acquisition.

Generally, with backend marketing you talk to people or send them a card or newsletter and the time and money spent cultivating the relationship with the people who already know you is less than fifty dollars. In turn, over the next seven to ten days that contact is going to come across other people who likely need what you have to offer. That person who knows you is going to talk you up and then make a referral. Thus, your cost of acquiring that new client is less than fifty dollars; the lowest cost in the hierarchy of marketing activities for your business. Use the power of word of mouth to your benefit, find ways to encourage your current clients to spread the word about your business and offerings to their network.

On the other hand, the cost of acquiring a new client from frontend marketing is much higher. Say you did some online advertising and you spent $300 for numerous people to click on your ad and go to your landing page, but despite lots of interest you only got one actual client. That results in the cost of acquisition being $300 for that one client.

Bottom line, to stabilize and balance your marketing budget, you must engage in a mix of backend and frontend marketing efforts.

Remember, it is always more costly to find customers to buy from you for the first time than to get known customers to buy from you again.

There are many different ways to break down marketing, but in its simplest format here is a breakdown of four quadrants to marketing:

- Backend Marketing – Referrals from Raving Fans:
    o Clients, Former Clients, Acquaintances.
    o 3 leads out of 4 = 75% conversion
    o Activities: Newsletters, Cards, Phone Calls, Emails, Texts, Video Messages
- Backend Marketing – Referrals from Professional Referral Sources:
    o Colleagues, Network Acquaintances.
    o 2 leads out of 4 = 50% conversion
    o Activities: Newsletters, Cards, Phone Calls, Networking Events, Sending them Referrals
- Frontend Marketing – Clients from Engaging with People & Educating
    o New Potential Customers
    o 1 lead out of 4 = 25% conversion
    o Activities: Blogs, Articles, Seminars, Webinars, Community Events
- Frontend Marketing – Clients from Advertising, Online Marketing
    o New Potential Customers
    o 1 leads out of 10 = 10% conversion

      o Activities: Print Ads, Facebook Ads, Google Ads, Online Directories, Community Directories, Direct Mail

The goal in creating a marketing plan is to spread out your marketing in the different quadrants which will help even out the higher cost of acquisition from the frontend marketing with lower cost of acquisition from the backend marketing.

Marketing Campaigns

Marketing campaigns are a set of activities designed to achieve a specific, measurable set of goals in terms of reaching out to your particular target market. The campaign has a theme that you then spread out over multiple channels to hit audiences in the different quadrants, as illustrated above. Sometimes you want to just hit a particular audience in a specific quadrant and other times you want to spread the word to everyone. For instance, you may have a campaign that would target other professionals so you could employ in a series of activities to engage your professional colleagues and network acquaintances.

For example, you may have a specific campaign directed to your "Mary" demographic. The main message in the campaign would be targeted to reach Mary organically throughout her day; advertisements in local school publications, reaching her through other parents or teachers during their extracurriculars and targeting Mary via newsletters. All avenues would convey the same message but be reaching her on varying platforms- all of these would support the overarching campaign

Think of it as having an idea and needing to get it delivered to various audiences. The delivery happens via different marketing vehicles, which are the mechanism for spreading the word. The marketing campaign is the messaging that is getting delivered via a battle plan. It executes a series of marketing vehicles in a specific sequence, with a set of messages that embody what you are trying to communicate. It is intended to meet the business needs (often in support of sales).

As you grow your business, you will develop more marketing vehicles to use. In the beginning, hone-in on four to five marketing vehicles and get good at delivering consistent messaging via each.

Crafting a Marketing Plan Which Drives Strategic Campaigns

The first step to crafting a marketing plan is to think about the types of activities that will get you in front of your ideal audience or the people who influence the decision making of your ideal audience. Does your ideal prospect use a lot of social media? Do they read print articles, online articles or blogs? Do they attend networking events? Who do they rely on for advice? Do those influencers to your prospect use a lot of social media? Do those influencers to your prospect read print articles, online articles, or blogs? Do those influencers to your prospect network? In other words, think of where your prospects and influencers are.

Second, identify marketing activities you like to do, but make sure you always push yourself to build out more great marketing activities to grow your audience and your reach. If you love to network and talk to people, plan in those activities if that is consistent with your prospects and influencers. If you would prefer writing, plan some writing activities to get you in front of your ideal audience. However, if those are not sufficient, push yourself to add in other marketing activities to fill out the campaign.

Next, start thinking of different ideas for messaging that resonates with your ideal market. This is where you go back to the work you did on personas and avatars and build upon their concerns and the solution you have. It is crucial to enter the conversations that are already going on in your ideal prospect's head. Frame it the way your target prospects would understand and resonate with it.

Next, outline different marketing themes that tie in with the messaging that connects you to your audience.

Finally, assess whether the plan you are considering is worth executing. What is the total addressable market or revenue opportunity? What percentage of penetration can you achieve with the campaigns you are identifying as a part of your strategy? Do the costs of those campaigns outweigh the profit you intend to make from winning the business by converting leads that the campaigns generate?

Here are a few examples for crafting a marketing plan for your first quarter:

January is a big month for New Year's resolutions. Tying into the transformation your ideal client wants, you could run a "New Year, New You" campaign. This type of broad message, "helping people move forward in the new year," could be delivered via all marketing channels you use (social media, newsletter, phone calls, word of mouth, cards, networking events, etc.).

Next, Valentine's Day dominates in February, but there is also National Single's Day on February fifteenth, as well as many other holidays you could use. Depending on your audience, you could go with a broad marketing campaign like, "Give the Gift of Love, Give the Gift of a Referral," and teach people how to refer business to you. You could be more targeted with something like, "So He Just Proposed – Five Things You Need to Do Immediately." That campaign might just be targeted to women, and if you were seeking a specific audience, you might use Instagram and Facebook to promote the campaign.

March is the heart of spring. You could focus on "Freshen Up for Spring" or something with flowers. On the other hand, if you have sports fanatics, perhaps you want to tie into March Madness and make some analogies about being proactive with your product and how to formulate a good offense rather than playing defense.

As you move toward the second quarter, you might want to start focusing on a campaign related to, "Getting Ready for Summer." This will resonate with the planners who are already planning months in advance. With this type of campaign, you could target parents, or perhaps you want to target the influencers, like grandparents, who might be willing to pay for a unique summer camp or some other experience.

The point of building out a marketing plan is to start layering in different opportunities to reach your ideal audience strategically. You start broad, think 10,000-foot view, then you get more and more specific with details at the 5,000-foot view (what marketing channels will you use, what messaging you will use), and then you will build in the 1,000-foot view with the exact ad or social media images and copy.

Tracking

With all marketing, it is absolutely imperative that you track what works and what doesn't work. Everything has to be measurable and in support of well-defined goals. Measurements have to be frequent enough to make real time decisions about your marketing activities. This way you know when you should change the marketing, increase it, decrease it, etc.

Start at the top of the funnel. Track the activities you do and how many people you touch, then track the metric of how many leads come from that activity. Next, track how many of those leads convert. Marketing must always convert to sufficient profitable revenue to justify doing in the first place. Always look for ways to improve marketing at all levels

If you track the entire funnel, then you can see where you may have a leak in your pipeline and all your leads fall out. Perhaps leads come to your landing page, but only one in 1,000 takes action from the landing page. That means you may need to tweak the landing page. Maybe 250 of the 1,000 take-action from the landing page but then they don't actually buy. This may be an issue with your sales process, the sales copy, or the sales conversation. Again, tracking this information gives you the data so you can make informed decisions on what needs to be changed.

Focusing on your ideal client and crafting a marketing plan takes work, but with the right systems in place that create, manage, measure and drive sales opportunities, the results are well worth the effort!

Chapter 8 Recap:

- Finding things you like to do and working with the customers you want to work with.
- Map out your ideal personas
- Create avatars to give you greater insight into their concerns, pain points and daily life so you can target your marketing appropriately
- Understand your costs of customer acquisition
- Balance your marketing plan with both backend marketing and frontend marketing
- Craft a marketing plan that drives strategic marketing campaigns
- Track all your marketing activities

Your Action Plan:

1. *Identify what your business does that is of interest in solving which problems you know your customers have*
2. *Construct your personas*
3. *Build out one marketing avatar*

4. *Map out your marketing channels*

5. *Brainstorm some marketing campaigns that interest your customers*

6. *Calendar time to craft a marketing plan*

7. *Create systems for tracking your marketing*

Kristen S. David

Chapter 9: How to Systemize Marketing so It Can Run Smoothly

A key to building a thriving, profitable, successful business that can run without you is building systems. First, identify regular activities and slowly take each one and automate it. You do this by creating a process so that it can either run on its own automatically or be run by people through the use of clear procedures and policies to use those procedures.

This is the part that isn't sexy to build, but it is *so worth it*! This is what makes your business repeatable. It is what lets people accomplish positive things for your business without your direct supervision thereby giving them a sense of personal contribution and shared success.

So, what are some of the types of marketing systems you can build?

- Newsletters
- Social media
- Email drip campaigns
- Direct mail
- Follow-up sequences
- Webinars
- Workshops
- Livestream events
- Networking

- Advertising – online
- Advertising – print
- And so much more!

Building Marketing Systems

The easiest way to build these systems is to document or record the step-by-step process as you are doing it. You can later clean it up but embrace that you are taking the first step and get at least the basic process down. Busy business owners often think it would be quicker to do it themselves, but this thinking will keep you stuck in the trenches and will not empower your employees. Find someone to help you and explain the process to them, layering in comments on how you want it done and tips for how to do it the right way.

As you grow, you will refine the process, add in more examples, templates, scripts, and other supporting resources to ensure it gets done the way you want it done. Done correctly, your employees will begin suggesting system improvements to you and thus make your business thrive!

If you want to get systems built fast, pick one to work on and spend several weeks documenting and refining the process. This is a bit more complicated when it is a project or marketing activity that is new to you as well. Talk to others or work with someone who has done it. Working with someone with experience with systems can shorten the process, so you don't have to reinvent the wheel.

A key to building reliable, working systems is to clearly articulate the following mantra in every procedure: *who* shall do *what* by *when*?

This provides clarity so that each person knows what they need to do and understands the clear deadline by when it needs to get done.

Story Time

As I grew my law firm, I hired a temp to cover the receptionist duties for a week while our receptionist took a vacation. The woman was wonderful in so many ways, but on Thursday we got a mysterious phone call from a gentleman wanting to change his appointment with me. I didn't know anything about the meeting; it was not on my calendar, and my secretary said she didn't know anything about it either. We went to the receptionist, and she knew exactly who he was. When we asked why it wasn't on the calendar, she said the procedure wasn't really clear, so she was waiting until the end of the week to add all the appointments at once to the calendar. My jaw fell open and needless to say I was dumbfounded. While yes, the procedure did not say calendar "immediately," it defied all common sense in my mind.

Lesson learned: we amended the verbiage in the procedure because one should never assume that another person knows what you are implying, and so you need to add detail when you discover a grey area in your systems that is open to interpretation.

Getting Buy-In from the Team

As you develop policies, procedures, and systems, it is vital to help your team understand why this process is going to help make their life easier. When you first introduce the concept of systems, be gentle and make sure they understand it is going to benefit everyone. The new process should make their jobs easier to do and give them the opportunity to make even greater contributions to the business that pays their salaries and provides their benefits. If your staff doesn't understand why something is being pressed on them, they will often stage a revolt.

Depending on your workplace culture and the leadership styles, you may want to invite the team to help you build the marketing systems. The best systems are the ones that people understand and believe in, and the best way to achieve that is to have them help document, design and, over time, evolve those systems. Then your staff gets to walk the talk. This also gets them into the mode of being "systematic," and that means that they'll design future systems, thus freeing up your time yet again. What you may find is that some of the people around you have hidden talents. They may be great at writing, which could lead to them helping with writing some of your marketing copy. Another staff member might be great with layouts, graphics, and videos for the policies and procedures, which could lead to their help with some marketing graphics and videos.

After your team assists you in crafting these processes, as the owner, your job is to ensure the system integrates with your mission, your core values and your culture.

Finally, it is essential to review them regularly and make adjustments as necessary. Your team will thrive when they know they have the opportunity to provide input and make a change as needed. They will also become more loyal as they see their contribution to the company steadily increasing through the use of systems that reduce their stress levels.

It may take a few days or a few weeks to build out the system with sufficient specificity such that a temp could handle the process, but it will be worth it. Remember, systems run the business, and your team runs the systems. Make good, strong marketing systems, and your business will run smoother.

Set a Plan for Building Your Systems

While tempting to say, "Let's build all of it immediately," that can sabotage getting any systems completed. Choose one every two weeks or every month, and spend some focused energy building out the system.

Each marketing process should have the policy (why are we doing this) and then lay out the process from beginning to end, with procedures written out for each step. Start with something that you are familiar with, like sending a newsletter or attending networking events. Be sure to document each step ranging from the prep work to the actual event to the follow-up. It is okay if these are not perfect right away. Get them drafted and start using them; you can always edit and perfect them later. When you complete them, note the date and calendar a review for thirty or ninety days.

Building marketing systems can often fall by the wayside as you are inundated with all the priorities pulling at your time but building these out ensure the prosperity of the business. In particular, they free you up so that you can more easily go and deal with all the priorities that are pulling at your time. They are both an investment in your business and an investment in your life, making both thrive over time.

Chapter 9 Recap:

- Identify regular marketing activities and slowly take each one and automate it by creating a system for it
- Build these systems by documenting and recording the step-by-step process so a temporary worker could do the task
- Get buy-in from the team through participation
- Regularly review and make adjustments as necessary
- Create a monthly plan for building the systems

Your Action Plan (so you can build the marketing systems which will give you the freedom to take vacations and allow your business to thrive without you needing to crack the whip at every step):

1. *Identify the marketing systems you want to build*
2. *Set your plan for building your marketing systems*
3. *Get team buy-in*
4. *Have regular meetings to assess if the system is still working or needs further refinement*

Pillar 3: Management

Kristen S. David

Chapter 10: Surrounding Yourself with a Great Team – Finding, Vetting and Onboarding Productive People Who Fit Your Culture

Surrounding Yourself with Great Employees

To build a successful team, you must find employees who are on board with your mission and the culture you created. Culture is how people work when you aren't looking; it is the ambience of productivity and excitement to do the things that will help the business move forward and help more clients.

It is important to align the interests of your business, with the interests of your team, and with the interests of your clients. In this way, everyone feels productive and as if they're moving forward in the same direction.

Productivity

The workplace is for productivity related to work. At the end of the day, there should be a sense of accomplishment from completing your work. It is essential to *establish priorities and keep the work moving*. We must instill in our team the mindset that if they find they have more work than they can handle, they need to meet with a supervisor and establish priorities. If your team feels overwhelmed and stressed all the time, they will get discouraged and will disengage.

My favorite productivity quote is from Dan Kennedy in his book, *The No B.S. Guide to Managing People*:

"Productivity is the deliberate, strategic investment of your time, talent, intelligence, energy, resources, and opportunities in a manner calculated to move you measurably closer to meaningful goals."

– Dan Kennedy

People want to feel they are moving forward, and it is imperative to set projects and goals so your team can feel they are productive each day. It is important to tell your staff what the goals are – you'd be surprised how often that doesn't happen! Whether it is a small achievement or a big one, a team that feels productive rather than spinning their wheels will stay with you longer and be more productive.

Culture

A strong culture can reduce overhead costs, reduce turnover, and increase profitability. A strong culture binds people together, essentially into a tribe or extended family that makes a lot of magic happen. Too often business owners ignore this crucial tool in building their team, and their business suffers as a result.

If we build a culture where everyone knows what is expected of them, how they fit in the overall organization, and that they will enjoy each day's work and feel productive at the end of each day, you are more likely to retain those great people. You are also more likely to lose any "problem" employees as the cultural will naturally deselect them and cause them to leave.

However, culture is not just the work attitude; it is also the overall image and feel that you want your business to portray in all ways.

Story Time

I had an excellent receptionist working in my law firm who started two months prior. She always dressed appropriately and professionally in smart business attire. Randomly one morning, she arrived for work looking as if she was about to go "clubbing." She had on an extremely short skirt, a crop top halter top, a large belly button ring, and her hair was "poofed up" more than her typical hairstyle. My jaw dropped open when I saw what she was wearing. It wasn't that what she was wearing was not acceptable for a woman to wear, but it wasn't acceptable for my professional law firm and the culture I was propagating for my team and my clients.

It was clearly not my finest hour when I blurted out "What are you wearing?"

No judgment folks; sometimes we say things we shouldn't when we are utterly astonished.

I ultimately sent her home to change and realized that I needed a real dress code policy so I would have something objective to reference when addressing outfits that were less than fitting for the law firm image I wanted to portray.

In contrast, consider a similar story from the point of view of a seasoned business owner who didn't react like I did above. He once came into the office to find they had a new receptionist who had orange hair in pigtails, a top hat, and combat boots. Rather than send her home (or fire her), they coached her a bit, and she figured out that though the dress code was relaxed, there were some rules. These days, she is the director of investor relations for a large company in San Francisco. She made it from receptionist to executive because the culture of the business and the owners allowed her to develop without swatting her down on that first day.

So, how do you build culture? There are entire courses on this for a reason, as it takes time to infuse and produce.

Building culture starts with the owner getting clear on the culture they want to build. There are dozens, each with a thousand variations, of workplace cultures, from hierarchy to collaborative. Culture is also coupled with the leadership style of the owner and the executive team. While everyone may have a leadership style they want to emulate, many owners exhibit different attributes in different moments. When things are tense, it can often be very authoritarian. When things are relaxed, it can often be more of a servant leadership or coaching style, where you help your team build, grow, and succeed.

Once you get clear on what you want to build, it then becomes necessary to assess the office environment, use the right tools, and engage your team in the right way. Internal trainings, performance reviews, and knowledge of the intrinsic and extrinsic motivators of your team are all crucial for building your team's culture. Your office environment, policies, and systems are also key to building a culture that resonates with both your customers as well as your team. Finally, the owner and the executive team must take the time to plan and set clear goals and key performance indicators (KPIs) so the team can have clear landmarks.

In addition, it is absolutely key that the owner and executive team must also be participants in the culture. They must walk the talk, or the rest of the company will think the culture is a sham.

Before you can find and onboard great people to fit your culture, you need to first establish what the culture of your business is.

Here is an exercise to help you get clear on what you envision:

- Is your business very uptight, rigid, and stiff, or is it laid-back, relaxed, and casual?
- Is your business dour/somber, or is it happy/joyful (or somewhere in the middle)?
- Is your business self-centered and driven, or helpful and willing to go the extra mile for clients?
- What does your advertising "say" about your business?
- What does your website "say" about your business?
- What does your front door "say" about your business?
- What does your receptionist convey about your business, in the tone and manner of answering calls?
- What does your lobby "say" about your business?
- What does your office "say" about your business?
- How do you and your people work? Are you productive each and every day?
- What do your clients say about you and your business?

The above likely made you realize that some changes need to occur in your business. If your company has messy offices with things everywhere, that sends a message to your team and your clients about the type of business you run. *Broken Windows, Broken Business* by Michael Levine addressed this concept, writing that when you fail to pay attention to the details, business problems will surface. In the case of broken windows, if left unrepaired, soon other windows will break, and soon the perception is that the owner doesn't care.

As the owner, you need to be a leader worth following. Pay attention to your culture and the details. You set *the* example all the time, whether you realize it or not.

Get clear on what you envision for your business. Formulate that vision into words so you can share that vision with others and make a plan to start making changes to align your office with the culture you want.

Who to Hire First, the GAP Analysis

Whether you have no staff or a staff of twenty people or more, the question always comes up, "Who should I hire next?" Does this sound familiar?

You must first enter into the hiring phase with a clear understanding of who you really need. To understand that, you need to perform a GAP Analysis. The GAP analysis has been around for quite some time and gives a good starting point to gain clarity on what staff members you currently have and who you need for the various open positions.

Here is how this analysis works:

- First, you write down the importance of every position in your business. Don't get caught up with the person who is or is not doing it yet. For example, the job of the receptionist (i.e. the responsibility of answering your phones and greeting customers); how important is it? Well, some would say it is crucial because that is the lifeline to new potential clients, so perhaps you grade this role a nine out of ten.

- Next, you note who currently does the job (hint – it might be you or someone else).

- Then, grade how well that job is being done on a scale of one to ten. Perhaps your assistant is doing it and not doing a great job because they are too busy with everything else, so you grade it a five.

- Finally, subtract how well this job is being done from the importance of the job. In this situation, we would use the equation: (9-5 = 4).

Now you go to the next position and grade it. After you have assessed all the jobs, you look for which ones have the most substantial gaps and further prioritize based on the overall importance. This helps you hone-in on who you need to hire first.

Finding and Vetting to Add the Right Person to Your Team

Once you know who you need to hire, it is vital to get clear on the job descriptions and who you need to fill the position. While many businesses spend lots of time on interviews, in reality if more time were spent crafting the ad using the job description, you would have better, more qualified candidates to interview. Take time to craft an ad that will attract the right kind personalities to fit your culture. Never be afraid to seek out someone brighter or more capable than you are. Encourage such people (so long as they are not prima donnas), and they will reward you.

Next, you need to market your company to attract top talent. This means writing a description to promote your company and convey the great culture, so the right talent wants to join your team. You also do this so that the wrong people do not apply. Give enough information about a dynamic, high performance organization which thrives on challenges, and this provides a natural deselection process for candidates that would be a waste of your time to interview.

Finally, you need a clear hiring process with criteria at each stage to truly hone in on the four key elements of what you want to learn about the person – education, experience, personality, and habits. You will discover the first, education, through a resume, but the second, third, and fourth need to be gleaned through the interview steps and reference checking.

Here is an example hiring process:

- Job Ad with Instructions.
- Written Interview
- In-Person Interview
- Check References
- Make an Offer

First, have candidates respond to an ad with specific instructions. This is the first way to see if a candidate can follow directions. Seriously, if they can't follow instructions when they are trying to get a job, it is never going to get any better! Even the minor task of having the candidate send their resume as a PDF or writing their name in the "re:" line can be a great tool to weed out quickly those who fail to follow instructions.

Next is the preliminary written interview. Before you invite the candidates in for an n-person interview, do an initial written interview asking them to answer some questions, send a video, or do some task that connects with the position. The questions or assignments should be written to help you further determine if the person has the skill sets (i.e. problem-solving, prioritization, organization, communication style, etc.) that will fit with the position.

The next step is the in-person interview. Compile your list of questions before the interviewee arrives if you genuinely want to find the right candidate.

Don't feel bad if you haven't been doing anything like what I am describing. This is a no-judgment zone – college and law school never taught me this stuff either. I wasted a lot of time and made some bad hires because I went with the flow and didn't use the interview to dig in. Remember, this is where you glean insights about how much experience they have, find out their personality (life is too short for a "glass half empty" person on your team), and see if they have good work habits.

Remember to take a look at experience. Prospects may have worked with a particular title, but we all know that the duties assigned to a title can change drastically depending on the workplace. A receptionist in one business may answer phones, handle mail, manage the CRM system, or manage multiple marketing projects like birthday cards, note cards, and referral gifts. In contrast, another receptionist many have never done anything but answer phones and transfer calls. Thus, while someone may not have all the experience you would like, consider if the person will be open to your teachings.

As discussed above, you want to find the right personalities and work style to fit your culture and the team you have in place. It is important to vet candidates to find the right fit. Changing a person's nature can take years, and as a growing business, you may not have that time. Take the time to assess how the person will fit with your team, how well you will be able to manage them, and what their goals and motivators are.

While you are interviewing, provide the candidate with enough information about your business and culture that they made decide to deselect themselves. Do not be afraid to ask the candidate if they feel they would be a good fit. Explore their answer and push on it as part of your own assessment of their fit.

For example, Hewlett Packard is a large, highly successful global multinational with a legendary corporate culture, knows as "The HP Way", that is a cornerstone of its worldwide business success. In its interview process, candidates are constantly asked at each stage in the process if the person feels they would fit and how they feel about "The HP Way". That is how HP keeps refreshing its workforce with people who fit and are committed to "The HP Way".

If that interview tactic works for HP, why not for your business?

Work style and follow-through is key to finding an employee that fits with your business. If you want to build a team that you are sure will always follow-through with every assignment, will be organized, proactive, and get the job done right the first time, you will want to ask some questions to glean more about their style and habits. Asking how candidates prioritize in the morning, what techniques they use to stay organized, and how they work with others to get a project completed can be very revealing. You can also ask them what three things they do, without fail, every week or month. Are your candidates quick to say they have great habits, but in describing these new habits admit they change gears thirty days later or do they stick with their commitments?

The next step is to check references. Hands down, this is the step most people don't take the time to do, and it can save you thousands of dollars. How would you like to save an extra $5,000? Great, pick up the phone and check references. Seriously, this can help you avoid hiring a crazy person who wastes a lot of time and money. (Imagine paying someone for several weeks or months when they can't do the job right, wasting your time and your team's time training them, answering questions, dealing with the chaos, and finally using the mental energy to fire them). Pick up the phone and call. Ask if their former employer would ever re-hire the candidate and listen to the tone of the response. This can give you a heads up if there is a massive problem brewing.

Once you are sure you want to hire the person, the final step is to provide an offer letter. Most business owners have every intention of getting to this but don't. At a minimum, draft an email or something that outlines the terms of the engagement, including that the position is subject to a background check or other elements allowed in your state. This gives the candidate a chance to make an informed decision if they too believe it is the right fit. If you want a good, productive employee who will be profitable, this is a must!

Finally, if you are new to hiring, do take the time to understand the legalities in your state. Go talk with an attorney and make sure you understand the rules of engagement.

Onboarding Plan

An "onboarding plan" may seem a bit scary, but it is relatively simple to map out in about twenty minutes if you know what the person is being hired to do. In addition to the usual HR onboarding briefing on benefits, employment practice at the company, etc., think about the core duties the person needs to learn in the first ten business days to truly learn the job. Then assign the person to learn one to two tasks each day and note how they are going to learn the tasks. For instance, a receptionist may need to spend the first day getting familiar with the business and start listening to the calls and the tone of answers. The person can also review the policies and procedures on answering phones, taking messages and triaging calls. Day two can focus on learning the phone system and starting to answer calls with supervision. Day three can change gears to learn about the processes for greeting guests and conference room duties (preparing for the guests' arrival, seating them, getting them water, clearing up after meetings, etc.). Finally, by day four, the receptionist should be answering phones regularly without constant supervision.

Be sure to assign who is going to teach your new hire these tasks and provide you with feedback on how the new hire is doing at the tasks and fitting in with the culture. Remember, your newest employee wants to feel useful and productive starting from their first day on the job, so plan projects and tasks that they can build on and get started on right away. Don't worry if your onboarding plan isn't one hundred percent complete on the first draft. Something is better than nothing. Also, the new employee can add to the onboarding list every time they have questions on how to do something that you can use as a reminder to incorporate into the planned onboarding process next time.

Finding and vetting new employees is an important process that can yield huge rewards by helping you onboard a fantastic team.

Surrounding Yourself with a Great Professional Team

The key to success is surrounding yourself with successful people. The alternative is to surround yourself with poor performers, and then you go out of business – or worse yet, you don't surround yourself with anyone, and you collapse!

There are several different categories of professionals you'll want on your team as you grow a successful business.

- Attorneys
- Bankers
- Business consultant/coach
- CPA
- Debt collector

First, you'll want trustworthy attorneys on your team. At various times while running a business, you'll need some dependable business attorneys to assist you from the initial formations of the business to help with navigating certain legalities. Find and retain a reasonable business attorney you can talk to so when problems arise, you can quickly jump on a phone call and get some answers and understand your options so that you don't go days and days fretting about a problem that might not truly exist.

You'll also want to develop a relationship with a good banker who will help you navigate and learn the nuances of setting up business accounts, and more importantly, starting to create business credit. This is important so that down the road as your business becomes more successful, you can get a line of credit, not through your personal credit, but through the actual business. A good banker can also help you with other options and information, including low-interest credit cards and streamlining ways for depositing and keeping your hard-earned money.

A business consultant or coach is another great asset to your team. While we all seem to know what we should be doing, what helps the most successful people to drive growth is having a coach on their team who helps them stay accountable to their goals and their business plan. Often, the most successful individuals have a variety of consultants because they know that it is better to seek advice from others than to presume they know best.

A CPA is another crucial member of your professional team. There are both financial CPAs and managerial CPAs. The first takes last year's data and processes it, as is the case for many CPAs out there. However, as you start growing and becoming more profitable, it is vital to work with an excellent managerial CPA who will help you plan and use tax strategies to assist you and the business. This can often result in thousands of dollars of savings, so finding a proactive CPA should be high on your list.

If you don't like following up on your old accounts receivables or people who have not yet paid you, you might want to get a good debt collector on your team as an outside vendor, so when those matters arise, you can quickly hand it over. It's nothing personal against the client; it's just that when a client contracted to use your services or work with you, they agreed to pay you, and you deserve to get paid for that work. Get your money.

Surround Yourself with Great Virtuals and External Vendors

You will also want to surround yourself with great virtuals and vendors to help with day-to-day operations, such as:

- Receptionist/virtual receptionist
- Office cleaners
- Bookkeepers
- Virtual Assistant
- Informational Technology Company

When you spend so much time marketing your business, the last thing you want to do is lose potential phone calls from new clients or individuals who can help assist in making your business better. You can use a virtual receptionist to flip the phones over and answer the phone when you are busy, or if you have to step away from the business for a day or two. One particular company that has done an excellent job for small businesses for years is Ruby Receptionists in Portland, Oregon. I remember my first visit to their offices so I could see how they do such a fantastic job. To this day, I remember how I was greeted by their customer relations team. The woman who gave me a tour of their offices took the time to show me not just how they do what they do, but also how they build the culture of their team and empower staff to send presents to their clients. I was in awe at how they would spend multiple days training their staff before ever letting them handle an incoming phone call. I was completely enraptured! As I grew my business, even when I had a full-time receptionist, it was great to let Ruby handle the overflow. This gave me the confidence as a business, that we were never missing important calls or leads. Before you spend more money on marketing, make sure your phones are being answered!

Next, ask around and get a reputable cleaning company who can come in once or twice a week, or more frequently if needed. Your time is precious, and you don't need to be taking out the garbage and cleaning the toilets when you could be otherwise making sales or planning out a successful marketing campaign. Take the time and invest in getting a respectable company to take care of this for you.

A bookkeeper is one of the most critical positions for your business. Remember, the financial numbers are everything at the end of the day. For most business owners, we are the overpaid, underqualified bookkeepers who never have enough time to really do bookkeeping. Find someone great who can zip through and do it right the first time, rather than trying to muck along and do it yourself. If you have a good bookkeeper, you won't need them a lot until your business gets busier, but it's essential to know that there's somebody who helps keep all the expenses and the financial matters in order. This is especially a huge time saver when tax time comes or if you need to go back to invoices or anything else from prior months. Be a good financial *manager* and manage the finances by using a good virtual bookkeeper – don't try to do it yourself.

As you grow your business, you simply don't have time to do all the little tasks that need to be done. Engage with a virtual assistant to help you with everything from travel plans to researching information to administrative tasks. When I ran my law firm on the west coast, I used to use a virtual assistant on the east coast so I could delegate lots of tasks before I left for the day and the next morning when I came in it was all already done. I loved this! Even if you have an assistant, consider having a part-time virtual on your team to help with overflow projects. It will stabilize your business and help you maintain your sanity.

Another key external vendor is a great Information Technology (IT) company. This is another area where business owners try to do too much of this themselves for too long. Again, no judgment zone. I used to climb under desks in my suit to reset the internet or reconfigure a printer for one of my staff. Having a team that can check on your system remotely and manage problems that come up is a huge saver for not just the owner but for numerous people on your team.

Surround Yourself with a Great Virtual Marketing Team

Having a marketing team made up of these positions will also help you immensely:

- Web developer
- Social media vendor/assistant
- Pay per click/SEO/internet advertising vendor(s)

- Copywriter
- PR company

To start building a strong marketing team, ask around and find a good web developer who will help you create what you need and stage it for growth over time. There are a lot of great individuals and companies out there, plus a lot of mediocre to poor ones as well. Look at the testimonials and ask for references before you sign on the dotted line. Also, have a candid conversation on what needs to get performed in stage one as you start out, versus what will get added in as you continue to grow. The key to success is having a solid plan.

You'll want to make sure that you properly vet social media vendors or assistants and train them to understand your business and your messaging. This person must comprehend what you're trying to accomplish in terms of how to resonate with your ideal audience and how to precondition your prospects to want to hire you. A good rule of thumb for social media is to post one-third of the time to educate about what you do, one-third of the time to resonate with your audience and one-third of the time have a call to action. With a well-orchestrated plan, a good social media consultant or vendor can reduce the impact on your time while presenting you as the Rockstar that you really are.

Get clear on what you need from a pay per click/SEO/internet advising vendor or consultant and interview two or three to find someone who will a) listen to your goals and b) with whom you can communicate well. This is another category where there are great vendors, mediocre vendors, and some pretty horrible vendors. Ask for references and get clear on what they will do each month before handing over your hard-earned money.

Hiring someone to copy write is also helpful for your business. Not everyone likes to write, and while some of us do like to write, as business owners we often don't have time. Enter the copywriter. Depending on your marketing plan, this can be a pivotal person to have on your team to ensure projects are completed and don't wind up on hold waiting for you to get the copy written. Reviewing copy is always easier and less time consuming than writing it yourself.

Some businesses may wish to employ a full-on PR company to navigate complex situations as well stay a step ahead of the game in keeping the right message out there. Make inquiries and vet vendors to find a company that truly listens to your goals and what you're trying to accomplish.

Surrounding yourself with a great team takes work, but hopefully this chapter gave you insights and clarity on how to proceed forward.

Chapter 10 Recap:
- Find employees who are on board with your mission
- Create a workplace filled with productivity
- Build the right culture
- Always know who you need to hire next
- Find and vet the right candidates (ability, experience and fit)

- Have a clear hiring process
- Position your new employee for success with an onboarding plan
- Surround yourself with a great team (both on staff and virtually)

Your Action Steps:

1. *Define the culture you want to build in your business*
2. *Identify who you need to hire*
3. *Map out a hiring process*
4. *Craft an onboarding plan*
5. *Consider what other professionals or external vendors need to join your team to position you for success*

Kristen S. David

Chapter 11: Cultivating Your Employees so They Thrive and Grow and Don't Want to Leave

It is human nature for every person to want to grow, learn, and thrive. As an employer, if you fail to give your employees opportunities to grow, both professionally and financially, they become bored or unhappy and ultimately leave for a different job. That is generally a very expensive, unplanned transition for a business owner to suffer.

One particular method for helping people always have an opportunity to move up is to put in place a process for how your team can grow by honing their skills or learning new skills. Quarterly performance reviews evaluate how your staff is doing and whether they need to hone their skills to do their duties to the best of their ability. Promotions provide opportunities for the person to step into a new position. Promotions may be vertical or lateral, and may or may not include a pay raise.

Keep in mind, an employee's base pay is being exchanged for them doing the job they were hired to do. Don't get confused with annual reviews, which are meant to assess pay raises, with performance reviews which give them a chance to grow and thrive.

Performance Reviews

It is imperative that you give your team feedback as to how they are doing, or else, at some point, they will quit. Think about it. Who wants to play a game in which they don't know the rules of engagement and they don't receive feedback on how they are doing?

In the book, *Thanks for the Feedback*, Douglas Stone and Sheila Heen outline three forms of feedback:

1. Appreciation: business owners need to show appreciation to convey that you see your team, you notice how hard they are working, and you observe what they do well. Appreciation can stimulate the employee to work harder and happier.

2. Coaching: your staff sometimes needs help clarifying where they need to focus some time and energy to grow and get better. They need your leadership and guidance to help them improve.

3. Evaluation: this helps the employee understand how they are doing. Are they getting an "A" or a "C?"

Each of these is crucial to keeping everyone in alignment. Imagine an employee who believes they are an "A" because they think they're doing everything correctly, based on their understanding of their "sphere of duties" in their mind. However, what commonly happens is that the employee's belief of the "sphere of duties" is slightly different than the employers. The employer's idea of the "sphere of duties" includes additional duties not in the employee's perspective of the responsibilities. What happens is that the two circles don't line up. The employee is doing things the employer doesn't want them to do and not doing other things they do want them to do. This is where the frustration begins and if not addressed, can cause the relationship to deteriorate quickly.

Quarterly performance reviews give the opportunity to provide evaluation and identify some coaching that can take place to help your employees succeed. The coaching can be via internal trainings, either by the team as a whole, one-on-one with the employee, or something the employee can undertake on their own, like reading or taking a course. External trainings should also be considered helping your team succeed. Getting them out of the office allows them to feel valued and sends the message that the business is committed to investing in its team.

It is also essential to use performance reviews as an opportunity to better understand each employee's intrinsic and extrinsic motivators. As Jill Geisler explained in *Work Happy,* as an employer, it is not for you to motivate your team. It is for you first to identify what drives the person and then put those motivators in front of the person, so they motivate themselves each and every day.

Some people are motivated by extrinsic motivators, like salary, bonuses, perks, benefits, titles, and praise. Others are motivated by intrinsic motivators that resonate with who they are. For instance, some employees are driven by the contribution to making a purpose. They might say things like, "I'm proud to have an impact and make a difference." Others might resonate with growing and learning, or others might value autonomy and having a choice and a voice in what they do. The key is for you to know what motivates a given employee so that you can provide that employee with the opportunity to become motivated in doing their job.

Performance reviews give you a chance to communicate with your employees, recognize their contributions and help them add to their skill sets so that they can thrive within your business. That will build a stronger team, so that your business thrives even more.

Promotion Opportunities

As we hire rockstars, we often find that they quickly showcase their amazing abilities that go well beyond the position for which we hired them. Sometimes that go-getter characteristic is accompanied by their desire to move ahead in life and move up by learning new skills. One opportunity we can give those rockstars is to provide an internal training mechanism to help them uplevel their skills so they can step into a new position.

It is vital to give them a framework for growth. Think of a pyramid. At the base are the foundational skills the employee would need to learn for the new position or tasks. As they ascend the pyramid, you would layer in the additional techniques and trainings to help them hone their skills until finally, they reach the pinnacle, where they can illustrate their complete competence. It is when they hit the full competence stage, we should be willing to give them a raise or change their title, or otherwise address their intrinsic and extrinsic motivators.

Whenever you've got something that you want somebody to get good at, or someone learning something new, think of what that looks like at the top, then work your way down. This gives you the framework to build them up.

Remember, the art of delegation is not shoving something down someone's throat. Rather it's building the person up with the required skills/experience and building up your own confidence that they have mastered those skills to know how to do a task correctly. You want to hand them the authority to perform a task because you believe and trust that they will succeed in that task. It is the same when you are building a plan to help someone grow into a new position.

Here are some steps to help you consider the pyramid for growth you need to build in your business for your go-getters:

1. Map out the position you think they might be able to grow into.

2. Talk to the employee and see if they are interested.

3. Let them shadow the job or some of the tasks to see if that is indeed what they would like to do.

4. Discuss with them again before agreeing on a training plan.

5. Engage in preliminary training.

6. Let them do the task with someone helping them.

7. Once we believe they understand how to do it right and they are illustrating they are doing it well, let them do several tasks, but all the while coming back to you or the trainer to confirm it is being done correctly.

8. Next, get them to the point where they can do about five to ten of these tasks or using this skill with minimal questions.

9. At the next level, they can do twenty of the assignments with only a few spot reviews.

10. The final hurdle complete the task twenty-five times perfectly.

Your go-getter employee has now met your standard, and you have complete confidence that they're going to be able to continue to accomplish this.

Depending on the nature of the tasks, this pyramid could take two to three weeks, months, or even years. Each task is different, and each human learns at a slightly different pace, so understand this will adjust according to the person.

Now, the above focus is on practical learning. However, sometimes there is an education component. Your employees might need to go online and watch a course to get a certification or might need other training or experience outside of what your office can provide. Again, it is all about building a clear pyramid for growth.

To take a closer look at how this gets mapped out, let's take a look at an example scenario. Let's say you own a small law firm and you have an administrative assistant who is a clear go-getter. She comes to you after a year and divulges, "It's always been my dream to become a paralegal."

You say, "You know what? Let's give you a plan. For the next quarter, let's have you learn these three items (summarizing records, creating chronologies, preparing pleadings), and see if you really like it. If so, we are going to build a pyramid for growth for you. We will outline a plan, and over the next two to three quarters, we can help you enroll in the paralegal certificate online, which takes about twelve weeks. After that, we will have you start training to hit one hundred percent competence in each element we need in our firm that we will outline. The firm is willing to support you in this; however, you would need to commit to three parts. First, the firm will pay for half of the paralegal certificate, and you will have to pay for half of the certificate. Second, you have to agree to work on the coursework on your own, as this is above and beyond your job, and finally, you need to agree that if something changes and you no longer want to do this plan, you let us know so we can modify the plan. What do you think?"

When you have these "A-team" players, you want to allow them to grow and move up in the company. Don't hold back or you risk the chance of losing them.

Chapter 11 Recap:
- Annual reviews are different from performance reviews
- There are three forms of feedback you need to give your employees
- Create a company where there are promotion opportunities
- Be intentional in creating pyramids for growth

- The art of delegation is building up an employee's confidence that they are doing it right and building up your own confidence that they know how to do the task
- Engage in conversations with your team.

Your Action Plan:

1. *Schedule quarterly performance reviews right now*
2. *Engage your team and make sure they are getting the feedback they need from you*
3. *Build a pyramid for growth for any employees that want to learn new tasks*

Chapter 12: When It Is Time to Say Goodbye

Fortunately, or unfortunately, not everyone will stay on your team and sometimes it is time to proactively work on a plan to allow that person to fly free and find a job for which they are more well-suited.

So how do you know when it is time to cut someone loose and what are some of the mechanical ways to get the deed done professionally?

Do They Need to Go?

There is an old proverb, "If you wake up more than three days in a row thinking about someone who is not your spouse, then they have to go." It's so true! I've had plenty of situations where I wake up, distressed about a staff member, and then I go into work and deal with it. If, despite attempts to make it better, your employee hasn't improved, well, that's a pretty good indication they need to go.

The same goes when you are working with virtual employees and vendors!

Now, this presupposes that you know your team, know their personalities, know what makes them thrive, and know what makes them cringe and you have worked with them to position them for success, and it is not working out. In other words, you, the employer, need to step up and first make sure you are doing what you need to do to create the right environment and cultural program to position your team for success. Yes, sometimes it is about the employee, but often it is about *you* and the culture you have created.

When a decision has been made, and you are ready to terminate, it is all about orchestrating the discussion.

Working up to the Termination

A key component to having a good team is clear job descriptions, a transparent onboarding process, reviews as they onboard, and quarterly reviews to give the employee clarity as to what they need to do to succeed in your organization. Coupled with your business culture and your ongoing trainings, the right person will thrive and grow. However, for a variety of reasons, sometimes an "A" staff member starts to spiral down. Sometimes we can have an honest conversation with a "B" or a "C" team member who used to be an "A," and get them back on track so they are highly productive and a thriving member of your team. Other times, an employee evolved and is no longer the right fit. It may be that there are other things going on in their life, or it may be that there are other things going on with the personalities in the workplace. Still, it may be that they're just ready for something new and your organization isn't their passion.

The job descriptions and reviews will give you the clarity to see if your employee needs to be cut loose. However, business owners should not do this as a drastic measure or an impromptu thought. Termination takes consideration and time.

Egregious Behavior

Now, let's be honest. If there's someone who is absolutely inappropriate and engages in egregious behavior, that's the time to cut them loose immediately. This kind of behavior is sort of like pornography – you know it when you see it. There are lots of different shades of gray, but when something happens, you'll know that it is the time for the staff member to be let go.

For example, early in my career, I was a young attorney, approximately twenty-five-years-old at that time and had only been practicing for about eighteen months. I had a wonderful paralegal who thought she knew everything. One day, I asked her, yet again, to make the same correction to a document that had gone through three prior revisions and the mistake was still there. As I placed it on her counter, I let her know it had to get perfected because it had to go out that day.

As I walked away, I heard her yell, "No!" As I turned back to look at what was going on, I spotted a stapler flying through the air in my direction.

As I leaned back a little to make sure I was out of the way of the stapler, I remember thinking, "F*&$, can I fire her?"

Just then she blurted out, "I'm sorry I forgot to take my meds," at which point I thought, "S*&#, can I fire her?"

See, law school never taught me how to manage people and what was permissive or not permissive bounds of egregious behavior. I walked into my office and closed the door and called a friend of mine who did employment law and learned that indeed, yes, I could fire her.

It is in these moments that sometimes we don't know what the right behavior or level of response is that can rise to the point of immediate execution, but I will tell you, trust your gut. If your employee's behavior seemed that far off, you're probably right. (Do check with your local laws and make sure you're in a state where that's permissible but trust your gut.)

Planning out the Termination – Be Ready with Plans, A, B, and C

If you want a smooth termination, plan it out, so you have absolute certainty of the elements and components to make sure it goes smoothly. In overview, you will want to do the groundwork to make sure you have the paperwork in place, the game plan ready, and that you've spoken with the key members of your team and your bookkeeper to make sure that you have everything prepared. After you do this, then you'll execute the termination. Finally, you'll tell the rest of the team.

First, you'll want to take a look at any documentation or information you have that illustrates that the employee is no longer the right fit. This might be from quarterly reviews, previous write-ups, or anything that may assist in justifying the grounds for the termination are based on legal, legitimate grounds. This written information will also help secure in your mind that they need to go.

Next, you will want to anticipate how this will play out. Is it imperative to be in control of the entire termination process? This is also a technique you will teach to others on your team who eventually will do terminations for you as your business grows. Let's go through several scenarios.

"Plan A" is that everything goes perfectly. You approach the individual, and you indicate that the job is no longer the right fit and that you're letting the person go. Your employee acknowledges that it's no longer the right fit. They sign off on the paperwork you present to them and they gather their things and leave. This is one hundred percent how we all would hope every termination would go, but that's not always how it happens.

"Plan B" is the "crying sob story". You need to be prepared for the event that your employee gets teary, starts crying, or begs for their position. You need to stand firm in your heart why that person is no longer the right fit for your growing business. You will want to practice some words so you're ready to respond. It's often useful to give them an opportunity to come back in two weeks and do a debrief if they truly want to better understand why you're letting them go, but for today, make sure your employee knows the termination is final and you need them to sign the documentation. If necessary, you may need someone else to assist you in getting them up and out the door. If they're sobbing uncontrollably or making a scene, you may very well put them in a cab or send them home and indicate that you'll have their belongings packed up and sent to them. In other words, have a game plan for how you would handle this.

"Plan C" occurs if your former employee swings the other pendulum and gets angry. You want to make sure you think through how to handle and diffuse the situation as best as possible. For someone who is getting angry and yelling, directing their eyes down towards the documentation by gesturing with your hand towards the document will often redirect their focus to what is on the paper. This can start to diffuse the situation. In this situation, also be careful with your body language. For instance, you want to be strong in the conviction that a decision has been made but not appear confrontational. Perhaps shift your shoulders slightly, so they're at an angle, and focus them to the papers you are asking them to sign and then direct them to the door. Again, if things get out of control, you'll want to make sure there's someone else who can step in and help to further diffuse and assist the person in departing.

I encourage you to play this out in your mind a few different ways to see how you're going to respond and what words you'll use. Have a script in place that you will stick to – no matter what. This way, if in the moment, any of the above occurs, you will have the opportunity to know the best course of action already and not be left trying to figure it out as you stand there.

Throughout the termination, you will want to have the correct paperwork and timing worked out as well.

In terms of paperwork, be sure you have all the correct legal and financial documentation prepared in compliance with your state laws. In some positions and scenarios, you need very formal termination documentation. In other situations, something that simply reads, "I agree to keep all business information confidential. I agree to return the keys. I agree to shred any information I have about the proprietary information of the business." Those are mundane items that they initial and sign off on, and it's not a big deal. Again, consult with an employment lawyer or a human resources specialist in your state to make sure you act in accordance with the law.

You will also want to think through when you're going to have the person in the office or what location the termination should take place. I have often had someone come into work thirty minutes early so I can have the person terminated and leave before everyone else arrives. I have also done it late in the afternoon, when everyone else is leaving and hold the person and let them know that they're being terminated, so they can gather their belongings and leave after everyone else has gone. Again, sometimes the egregious nature requires that the termination happen midday, or in less than convenient times, but if at all possible, try to strategize and plan the termination.

If time is not of the essence, you'll also want to think through whether or not it's best to keep the person on for a few more days for a project or to complete a particular task. However, be cautious that this can be a slippery slope. If a person needs to go, they need to go, and you need to make it happen.

The Day Has Come – Executing the Termination

The day is finally upon you. Do something that helps you be your best self before, if at all possible. For example, head to the gym, swing by your favorite coffee shop, whatever would make you more relaxed and happier – do it. The point is, when you bring good positive energy to the table, it helps make the entire conversation go much better.

Next, make sure you feel comfortable about how you will open up the conversation. For some, the conversation starts with, "A decision has been made." For others, this conversation begins with, "The time has come." I know on more than a few occasions, when I had to fire an individual I liked, I started with, "As a business owner, we have assessed the position and the position needs someone else." That has helped a few situations where I really got along well with the person on a personal level, but they just weren't doing their job. Whatever stance you take to begin the termination, you need to take control of the conversation. You are not entering into a discussion with your employee where they can negotiate; you are executing a termination – follow the process and the script.

For good employees who are leaving for personal reasons, or upon a mutually agreement that they are no longer the right fit, sometimes you can allow them to continue for a week or two or give them letters of recommendation to assist them in finding other employment opportunities. Part of the leadership of a business owner is recognizing that some people on your team need to fly and you can help give them wings by giving them those opportunities in a leg-up to do other things. Again, terminations don't always have to be brutal.

If you took the above planning steps seriously, then the actual act of termination will be rather easy. You will not need to deviate or draw it out if you've got a well thought out plan. Letting someone go is never enjoyable, but these steps can help prepare you for the necessary terminations.

Telling the Rest of the Team

As with the planning of the termination, you'll also want to plan out how and what you say to your team. Particularly when there's a strong culture in your business, there may be some employees on the team who feel hurt that a team member was let go or feel it was unjustified. On the other hand, depending on the work product and circumstances, the team may feel relieved that this person is no longer part their workforce. Be very careful to respect the exiting employee's privacy and legal rights with respect to any information disclosure beyond simply saying they are, or have left, your employment. Be sure to bring a positive picture to the future of the company and what you believe this company can achieve with this team. Reiterate to them your intention to be fully vested in finding the right team members to add to the team in the future so that everyone can thrive together.

You may also wish to invite individuals to come chat with you and to give you further feedback about you having let this former employee go. This is often an opportunity where staff will open up and tell you about concerns of others or why they don't feel the person was rightly terminated. As an owner, I would much rather understand what's going on in the minds of my staff, so that I can course-correct, both in terms of general culture, but also address any situations that have started to get out of control. You will also learn some key information about how your team sees the culture and if they noticed a problem or why they didn't come talk to you about that problem sooner. Again, this can be a great opportunity to gain valuable information to help cultivate your remaining employees.

Chapter 12 Recap:

- Determine if the employee, virtual or vendor is no longer the right fit for your team
- Work-up whether the person needs to be let go immediately or if there is an opportunity to repair the situation
- Preplan how you will handle the termination with plans A, B, and C
- Strategize the termination so on the day of execution it goes smoothly as per your plan and your script
- Plan how and what you will say to the rest of the team

Your Action Plan (for when you need to terminate someone):

1. *Make the decision*
2. *Plan out the entire termination*
3. *Execute the termination*
4. *Tell the rest of the team*

Chapter 13: Supporting Your Team and Business with the Tools They Need

As you grow your business, it's important to remember that your people and your business will need the right tools for it to run at peak performance. If you withhold those tools, you make it more difficult, and you can sabotage your own growth. Let's break down a few of the ones that are common in every business.

Physical Workspace

Not everyone will have a brick and mortar building, but even if you work virtually, you need to have an area where you can work and be productive. I take my laptop on-the-go plenty, but I always know how to set up myself to have my computer, some water, and the tools I need so that I can be at my best. If you do indeed have a physical space, it's imperative to give people enough room to be able to do their jobs.

In fast accelerated growth, there are plenty of times when you have more people than you have space for and people are willing to work for a short period in cramped conditions, but ultimately they'll quit performing at their peak if you don't remedy that situation.

Tales from the Trenches

I once worked with a business owner in a business plan workshop, and he couldn't understand why his people had all of a sudden quit performing like they used to. As we dug in and unraveled the recent transitions, we found that he had added three more people to his team of three people, thus doubling the number of people, but without increasing any of the workspaces. We ultimately found he was having six people work in what was, in essence, one central office. No wonder people no longer wanted to work at peak performance. He moved and expanded, and his people immediately went back to being highly productive.

Office Environment

This is something that needs to be consistent with your culture. In fact, it's a complete trust-buster when you tell people your mission is to be innovative and cutting edge or utilize technology, and you walk into the office and there is a fax machine still sitting there, and you require people to write handwritten phone notes for every incoming a phone message.

Your office space, equipment, and furniture can have a lasting impression, not just on your team, but on your clients. If you're a brick and mortar traditional, that's fine. If you're cutting edge, that's fine. Think about what your business stands for and make sure the equipment, furniture, and technology are consistent with the brand and culture you want to build.

Computers and Technology

Technology evolves every single quarter. Successful businesses plan to purchase or upgrade on a regular cycle. Some schedule computer and technology updates every month with small technology purchases each quarter. This can help regulate the budget to ensure you have money there for when you need it.

For computers, your IT person may be able to just add some components to make it run faster and more efficiently for your team. However, in today's day and age, you likely will need to be looking to replace every couple of years. It's much better to replace a little at a time than to have to replace seven computers all in the same month. Yikes, that's a big cashflow dig.

While we're on the conversation of technology, talk to your team. Find out what other programs, apps, or components they have utilized in previous jobs. They may very well have some suggestions for some good programs that can help simplify and streamline your workflow processes and help the team communicate better. The caveat to this is, don't go crazy. No one wants to have to show up to work and open eight different apps just to get their morning routine completed. If you are going to make some transitions, it's necessary to have a "technology transition game plan." I would suggest you map it out in four stages:

- Stage 1: Investigating the product
- Stage 2: Ensuring your staff's buy-in
- Stage 3: Implementation
- Stage 4: Review and Debrief

First, investigate and review the product to see if it is truly the right fit for your business.

During the second stage, make sure your team is on board before you purchase. This means you must sell your staff on the idea that this program is going to make their lives better. The fact is, your team will never fully use it and embrace it unless you have this buy-in. This is the most common problem we see with technology. The business owner or administrator shows up with a new product and shoves it down the throat of the team; months later, it still isn't being fully utilized. This is directly cutting into productivity and profitability. Take the vital step of getting your staff's buy-in, and you'll have a much more productive, profitable team.

The third stage is implementation. This may include your administrative team spending a week or two importing or updating the system with key information, so it's usable for your team. Then engage with some training for two to three weeks if it's a smaller program and a longer duration for a larger program. Allow your team to stand up and teach others and show them what techniques or mechanisms they've used to help remember shortcuts and how to use the technology. Again, your team will have more buy-in if indeed they see that their own team is embracing, sharing, and working well with the new technology.

Finally, review and debrief. With many products, you always test, review and decide if you need to pivot, tweak, change it, or proceed forward with it. The same is true for implementing software and technology. Don't forget this key step, so you get input from your team and recognize how you might be able to use it better. If you're going to pay for technology, computers, and software, make sure you're getting the most out of them.

Outsourcing

This could be a topic all of its own, filling an entire book. In the business world, there are so many ways in today's day and age to outsource. In fact, some people who run virtual companies outsource ninety percent of what they do. It's important to make a list of things that can help you and be clear with your team when they can reach out and have others do this work.

Here are some suggestions of where you might want to outsource in terms of management to help you streamline:

- Virtual assistants
- IT Support
- Transcription
- Printing
- Mailings
- Birthday cards/Thank you notes/other cards
- Errands
- Designers

First, virtual assistants are imperative to being able to get things done when you and your team don't have time.

Next, there are lots of transcriptions options. It's easy to dictate, hit the save button, then send it for transcription and have it returned in a short period. Record and transcribe everything. If it's a long training, seminar, or speech, you might want to get the automated, computerized transcription at a lower rate, but for day-to-day ten to fifteen-minute recordings, have the quick turn transcription and save yourself time.

Printing is another area you can outsource. Many printing projects are quicker and easier to have someone else do. Develop a good relationship with a local printer or find someone on your team who knows how to send to a printing company and allow them to do the legwork.

Mailings can also be time-consuming; it takes a lot of time to print letters, insert them into envelopes, label them, stamp them, and get them out the door. Outsourcing can be a huge time-saver for you and your team, which can allow you to make more sales and more money. Price this one around and weigh the pros and cons of cost versus time savings.

As for birthday cards, thank you notes, or other cards your business sends out, it is easy to use a variety of online card companies to customize and send out a card without hassle. There are many different programs out there, so find one you and your team like and make sure everyone on the team knows that it's accessible to them so they can send birthday cards, get well notes, and other cards to acquaintances, business colleagues, and clients. This is how you 5X your marketing very quickly. People love receiving a card, and it makes your business stand-out in a positive, memorable way. For small businesses with not a lot of time, outsourcing the sending out of these types of cards would be one of the first marketing areas to check out

We waste a lot of time running around town doing different errands. In today's day and age, there are many apps and services that will allow you to pay someone else to run around and do those tasks.

Before you "tsk-tsk" the idea of paying someone sixteen dollars an hour to pick up your dry cleaning, go to the grocery store, or do other things, think about what an hour of your time is worth, because that's how long it will take you to get in your car, go to the places, do the shopping, get back in the car, and drive back to work. Your time is your most precious asset, so use it wisely.

It's great to have a good designer on your team. Using someone who knows you and understands your brand, can significantly shorten the turnaround time. It might be more marketing-related, or it might simply be a branding move to hone your image in everything the firm does. Again, having people on your "outsource team" ready and available is huge for getting things done when you are in a time crunch.

Chapter 13 Recap:
- Make sure your team has adequate workspace
- Ensure that your work environment fits your culture and your marketing message
- Stay on top of computer and technology updates
- Plan out your technology transition game plan for any new software.
- Outsource wherever possible to ensure your precious time is protected.

Kristen S. David

Your Action Plan:

1. *Review your physical or virtual space needs and identify a plan for any necessary improvements over the next twelve months.*

2. *Take inventory of your office environment and what may need to be changed to build out your ideal workplace culture.*

3. *Create an upgrade plan for your computers and technology and take into account a transition game plan, if necessary.*

4. *Identify tasks that you might be able to outsource and determine a criterion for when to send it out.*

Pillar 4: Financials

Kristen S. David

Chapter 14: Profitable Owners Are Good Money Managers

Some people are great with numbers, and some people are not. Some people love to dive into spreadsheets, and others do not. Some people like to run calculations and see how numbers play out, and some people do not.

Like it or not, as a business owner, you have a responsibility to track and review your numbers. Even when the numbers suck, it feels better to know what they are and be able to create a plan to meet your delta. Successful businesses make decisions based on the numbers. That is why it is imperative that you understand what the numbers mean so you can then make appropriate decisions. If you simply look at a bank balance, you might freak out, not realizing what has or hasn't been paid. On the other hand, you might look at that same bank balance and be ecstatic because there's lots of money in it, not knowing that tomorrow ninety percent of that money is gone with all the outgoing expenses.

When you're a good money manager, you send a message, not just internally to yourself, but to your team and your customers, that you respect and value the money that flows through the business and that you are doing your best to make sure it's not squandered away. Therefore, while this may not seem like it initially, it's a giant marketing message.

Have you ever been at one of those evening socials and heard someone complaining or telling a story about how their boss doesn't pay attention to the money? Yeah, you don't want to be one of those bosses. So, let's talk about what you could do to be proactive with the numbers. When you map out your goals, and you know how you're going to get to those goals, this allows you to have a value for which to compare your current status. This clarity can tell you if you're on track or if you're not on track.

The numbers will also help you understand both lag metrics and lead metrics. Lag metrics are things like last month's P&L statement or how you did in the previous six months; these are metrics that lag behind and only tell you in hindsight what has happened. On the other hand, lead metrics are things like how many consultations you're booking and based on your historical conversion rates, how many sales you anticipate. These numbers will then give you a prediction of how much revenue will be coming in the door. Don't get overwhelmed with all these components just yet; we're going to break them down and help you become a good money manager.

Before we can start discussing the numbers and what to do with those numbers, we have first to understand the critical financial reports that are going to give you the data. A good bookkeeper should be able to set these up for you, and you should get them on a regular, consistent basis.

Key Financial Reports

P&L = Profit and Loss Statement

This statement can be provided as a monthly report, year-to-date, per quarter, or in any number of different ways. It starts with a listing of your various income-producing sectors, then continues as a listing of all of your expenses by categories. This is called your Chart of Accounts. The key is understanding what is in each category. It's also good to use a numbering system, so the categories don't just alphabetize but appear in an order that makes sense to you. Create the categories into sections that make sense for you. Here are common ones in the business world:

- Payroll: for many business owners, this is your most considerable expense. You want to be able to see that subtotal so you can see what percentage of your overall revenue is going to payroll. If you don't have employees, you can easily categorize all your virtuals and contract workers into a section to get a clearer picture of this expense.

- Occupancy/office space: for some, this is another significant expense. For others, it's less. In theory, this should be somewhat static, meaning it doesn't change from month-to-month. But again, you want to see what percentage of your revenue is going to this category. In New York City this percentage could be 20-25%. If you run a virtual company, this percentage could be less than 1%. What is key is that you understand what your number should be and align it with your business.

- Marketing: this can be a rather broad category, so it is helpful to create subcategories. This will help you better understand how much you're spending on advertising versus networking, referral gifts versus promotional materials, website maintenance versus online marketing, plus other marketing expenditures. Again, the key is understanding what is in each category.

- Overhead: this is another broad category that can have many subcategories. It can be broken down into subcomponents, such as office expenses, computers and software, dues and subscriptions, printing/photocopies, communications (phone/cell/internet), furniture, equipment, postage/delivery service, tools, etc.

- Professional fees: these are often legal fees, accounting fees, license fees, etc. They can be broken down into subcategories or simply lumped together.

- Professional development: this can include coaching, training, books, workshops, and other expenses related to help you and your team uplevel their skills.

- Costs of Goods Sold: For many businesses their inventory spend can be substantial as well. For others it ebbs and flows. Take the time to make sure all expenses related to this category get properly categorized so you have a true figure for your monthly spend.

- Other regular expenses that relate to your business: for many companies, bank merchant fees are a key monthly expense. Sometimes there are costs associated with the goods or products you sell. Insurance should be an expense category that is there to protect you and your business. Travel is another common category.

The purpose of a P&L is to help you understand where your money is going. Many people just see money come in and money go out without taking the time to see where it is going. Getting solid on your expenses and your P&L will allow your analysis of your numbers to go much more smoothly.

Balance Sheet

This is the second most important document because it tells you your assets and your liabilities. The name of the game is to build assets and build up equity as you're working so hard building your business. Don't get frustrated if at first the numbers seem askew. Your balance sheet can look very different depending on the time of month the report is run. If it is printed just before the bookkeeper pays the credit card bill, it might show a huge expense of liability; if it is printed the day after you pay the credit card bill, it might show your business is looking great. The goal here is to review your balance sheet every month on the same day so you have a better understanding of what the numbers should be and can make a plan towards profitability and where you want to go.

In sum, your balance sheet provides you with a snapshot of your company's financial position and what the company owns and owes. It covers cash, physical assets, inventory, as well as debts. If your business has shareholders, this is where their equity is also reflected.

Budget and Budget Variance Report

Once you have your P&L established, it is easy to create a budget. Your budget is essentially your business plan in numbers through forecasted revenue and expenses. If you plan to hire next quarter, the budget should show the additional expenses, not just in the payroll and payroll expenses, but also a little increase in things like computer software, office expenses, and professional development. If you plan to increase your marketing to bring in more cash flow, you will budget a little extra money for marketing, but then you can also estimate/ project an increase in revenue. Causes lead to effects. Find the effect you want (hiring, more cash flow, better technology), then identify the cause and document that expense (increased payroll, increased marketing spend, increased technology spend).

Your budget variance report is simply a tool to help you see if you are on target in your plan. The report compares your actual spend with what you anticipated in the budget. If you are one hundred percent dead-on, then you are on track to your goals. If you are above or below, the key is to ask why it is off.

Typically, your budget variance report is generated weekly or monthly, depending on the cash velocity of your business. Budgets/forecasts are usually revised each quarter. That way you have
124

a set of stable business targets/goals (i.e. the Budget) while you manage your performance. This helps you steer toward those targets/goals on a more granular basis, and allows you to respond quickly to changing trends in your business.

Accounts Receivables Report

For many businesses, it is essential to keep a close eye on your accounts receivables (AR). An AR Report will show you the list of all of the people who owe you money. An Aged AR Report will show you who hasn't paid you in the last 30 days, 30-60 days, 60-90 days, and 90+. For many companies that bill for their services, it is vital to review AR and immediately contact anyone who is more than 30 days outstanding. Don't wait until it is 90+ days old and stinky. Get on the phone and get your money. This is part of being a good money manager. This is part of ensuring you never have any unpleasant cash flow surprises.

Accounts Payable Report

For many, it is helpful to get a listing of what invoices the business needs to pay so you can better gauge how much money you need. This can also be helpful if you have a lot of vendors and recurring expenses to track. It can also be used to prioritize to whom you pay out cash and when you make those payments – again to avoid any unpleasant cash flow surprises.

Daily Posted Cash Report or Deposit Detail

This report can give you an updated look at what revenue has come in and hit your accounts. Once the business is running smoothly,

125

this report can be a boost to your day and help you feel the heartbeat of your business. Cash flow is king, and this is the report that tells you how you are doing.

Depending on the nature of your business, these are other reports that may very well be key to the success of your business. Work with your financial team to find what is vital for you.

Work in Progress, Inventory and Inventory Aging Reports

For businesses who use physical inventory, you will want to ensure you get these reports on a regular basis. They cover inventory on hand, inventory dedicated to product or services orders (work in progress), missing inventory (i.e. supply chain management issues) and how your inventory is turning (i.e. inventory aging and the cycle in your business – which effectively ties up working capital). These can be instrumental for spotting problems before they get out of hand,

Working with Your Financial Team

Key members of your financial team are:

- Bookkeepers
- CPA
- CFO

As we discussed when building your professional team, having a good bookkeeper can make a huge difference in your ability to get your numbers and understand your numbers. Most people try to do the bookkeeping themselves and suck at it. Get a good bookkeeper who you can talk to and who will help you plan for growth. Once you have a good bookkeeper, set up weekly appointments to speak with your bookkeeper to go over questions, concerns, and tasks that need to be addressed.

You need a good CPA (certified public accountant) on your team, preferably someone who owned, or still owns if a contractor, their own business and understands business ownership and propelling growth with profitability. If profitability is a key goal for your business, you need to find a good CPA who also understands this concept and doesn't sabotage your every attempt to plan out profitability. You also want someone who's going to help you strategize and tax plan to position you in the best situation possible. Too many CPAs simply look at last year's numbers and process returns. An excellent managerial CPA will help you forecast and manage the growth of the business, not just take what happened in the past for granted.

In addition to a CPA, you will want a good CFO (chief financial officer) or other coaches to help you review your financials and ensure that you are planning sufficiently. A good outsourced CFO can be a great addition to your team until you get to the stage of growth where the business needs a full-time CFO. This person will easily pay for themselves as they help you save money and maintain your sanity. Your CFO not only makes sure the CPA and bookkeeper are building and using good systems within your business, but also advises on financial strategies such as establishing your internal return on investment requirements, lines of credit, capital loans, investments and, as you develop the necessary cash flow, acquisitions you might entertain to accelerate your business' growth.

Finding time to review the financial information can seem daunting at first, but with just a little bit of effort, this can be one of the most manageable parts of your week. If you've got all your key information and you understand what these reports say, it's easy to sit down and do a quick review and course-correct as needed. Ideally, set one to two hours aside to review this per week, especially as you're getting familiar with managing the business by the numbers. Eventually, when you become familiar with the reports and your business' natural operational pulse, this can go down to half an hour a week, once the system is working well.

Build Financial Systems

As you and your financial team learn to process the financial information, build out the documented systems so if your bookkeeper, or a key individual on your financial team, leaves on vacation, the whole firm doesn't come to a screeching halt. A mini-library of videos and screencasts to accompany the procedures can be a godsend if an emergency arises and your bookkeeper is off-grid. This element of building systems is what ultimately makes the business more stable and shows that you are a good money manager.

Each month tackle one area and document why you do the task and then step by step how to do the job. Or address this by quarter. Quarter 1: money coming in (accepting money, depositing money, etc.), quarter 2: money going out (accounts payables, budget, budget variance reporting, etc.), quarter 3: monthly and quarterly bookkeeping duties (reporting, payroll, reconciliations, etc.) quarter 4: forecasting (cash flow projections, estimated sales, etc.).

Chapter 14 Recap:

- Successful businesses make decisions based on the numbers
- Key financial reports allow you to understand the heartbeat of the business
- Work with your financial team and get their help
- Build financial systems to stabilize and protect your business

Your Action Plan:

1. *Review your key financial reports and talk to your financial team if you don't understand them*
2. *Set up weekly, bi-weekly, monthly, or quarterly meetings with each person on your financial team, depending on your business needs*
3. *Start building financial systems*

Kristen S. David

Chapter 15: Money In and Money Out

First, you have to understand what money is coming in the door. Then you *must* be a good money manager and determine what percentage of your money goes out the door and what money stays in the business (and self generates to become profit in your pocket.) Many of us want to grow fast, and that is great, but you have to grow with a plan, and you need to carefully choose how your money goes out the door.

Assessing Your Financial Reports

The 3 x ROI Principle

In general, you want to make sure you are getting at least a three-time ROI (return on investment) on each expenditure. For some expenditures, that is easy to see. For instance, on a marketing expense, you might see a straightforward correlation between the ad or marketing expense and multiple new clients. You take the average value of those clients in terms of revenue and see if it equals at least, if not more than, a 3 x ROI.

For instance, a $500 print ad might yield three clients that are each worth $800. Thus, the $500 spend resulted in $2,400 of revenue or a 4.8x ROI. Other times, the marketing spend may be a blend of goodwill and brand awareness. Take, for example, a $1000 sponsorship; it provides the opportunity to get in front of 5,000 potential customers who will see you as a community partner. While this won't yield a direct ROI initially, the hypothesis may be that it will generate an ROI over time, since you are likely to get some referrals or clients in the months after.

It is good to review and analyze your spending every six months to ensure that each expense is still serving your business needs. It is sort of like the gym membership that gets purchased and forgotten about or the online subscription that is "out of sight, out of mind," and you keep paying for several years before you finally cancel. If you want to run a profitable business, make sure your expenses are working for you and generating profitable revenues.

Benchmarking Your Spending

A significant tool to driving up your profitability is to assess your current spending by category in terms of percentages to overall revenue and then map a plan to get to the type of percentages you want so the business has a higher profit.

For instance, if your marketing spend is currently twenty-four percent of your overall revenue, and your payroll is running at sixty percent, and your rent is nine percent, that means you only have seven percent left to pay all the other expenses of the business. That doesn't leave much of anything for profit.

As a business owner, it is hard to hold this analysis and make a plan if you don't know your numbers and if you don't know the percentages that are going into your categories like payroll, marketing, overhead, professional fees, professional development, etc. If you want to take control of your businesses and increase profit, that analysis is vital.

Story Time

I was working with a medical professional who couldn't understand why her business was generating about $100,000 a month in revenues, but her bottom-line income was negative each month. We took the time to map out all of her spending and calculated the percentages by category. There is something about black and white numbers that tell a very telling story without the need for words. As we reviewed the benchmarking spreadsheet, she could immediately see where spending in specific categories was vastly more substantial than what she thought. We were then able to discuss what the percentage ranges should be and craft a plan to align the spending over the next three quarters.

As she and I did in that example, take the time to map out your spending and set your benchmarks, so you have a clear milestone to hit.

Profit First

Enter profit first. As discussed in the early chapters of this book, there is a concept that is becoming more and more widespread throughout the business community called, "profit first." In his book, *Profit First*, Mike Michalowicz set out a straightforward methodology to get clear on the profit you want, subtract it from revenue, and then allocate the remainder of the funds for paying various expenses in a planned pattern. If you are tired of being a slave to your business and not taking home money, it's time to jump on board.

In addition to allocating profit off the top, Michalowicz also recommends setting up additional categories to pay yourself, money for taxes, and other vital components that you need. At its heart, this is all about building a financial plan and sticking to it.

If you want profit and you are not currently getting it, you either need to spend less or make more money.

Course Correction – A.K.A. How to Ramp up Profitability

For most business owners, there are a variety of ways to increase profitability. The "five R.U.L.E.S of profitability" have been around for some time and give focal areas to work on to increase profitability in your business.

- R (Rates): If you increase your rates and provide more value, you can increase your profitability and increase the happiness of your clients.

- U (Utilization): If you can increase the productivity of your team and fully use each person, this is another excellent way to increase profitability since you are effectively lowering costs through increased performance by the same staff. A quick way to find improvements it to ask yourself or your team, where are you losing time doing low-level tasks that can be delegated or streamlined with technology or better processes. Often individuals jump in and do tasks to help out, but they are not always the best person for the job, and it can suck up a lot of their energy and time. Make sure you are using each person for the tasks they are best suited to work on.

- L (Leverage Technology): If you use technology to help streamline your workflow and processes, you can often reduce time and cost, which will increase profitability.
- E (Expenses): You need to watch the money going out the door and make sure each expense is working for you. Cutting expenses that no longer serve you can boost your profits.
- S (Speed of Collection): The faster you can get your money, the more profitable your business will be. That is because you are losing money when you or someone you are paying has to follow-up and get paid. Get your money and boost your profits.

Set Quarterly Goals to Increase Profitability

A key to increasing profits is to make a plan each quarter to tackle one area and improve it. If you can, increase your profits by one to two percent each quarter by better utilizing your team, leveraging technology, any of the R.U.L.E.S., or any other technique that works for your business, this will put you on a path to success.

Chapter 15 Recap:
- Assess your financial reports
- Benchmark your spending and set milestones to achieve the benchmarks

- Engage in Profit First
- Understand how to ramp up your profitability
- Set your quarterly goals to improve profitability

Your Action Plan:

1. *Assess your expenses and ensure that each is working for you*

2. *Perform a benchmarking analysis on your P&L and pay attention to where your percentages might need to be reduced*

3. *Engage in "Profit First"*

4. *Make a plan to increase your profitability quarter by quarter*

Chapter 16: Planning Growth and Scalability

Growing and scaling means building out the plan and seeing how you will get yourself and your business to that next level. Understanding the plan and the potential pitfalls are key to your success.

Long-Term Planning

While we talked about long-term planning earlier in this book, by now you probably have a better sense of what you want to build and what you need to do to get there. It also likely gave you insights into how you can systematize your business so you can lead your team and your business to the next level

As your business grows, you will onboard additional team members to help you manage the business, perhaps a chief operating officer, a chief financial officer and other C-suite level staff. Letting go and allowing those other qualified individuals to run your business is often a hurdle that some business owners just can't seem to overcome. In your mind, start preparing for the day when you are not calling all the shots. Get curious and excited about how amazing it will be – that is if you want to grow to that level.

Perhaps you don't want a large team, you just want to grow and scale through more automation and outsourcing, and that can work too. Or perhaps you want to scale by acquiring other businesses – a perfectly fine way to grow if you have the capital and management talent to make the acquisitions. The point is you need a conscious plan and you have to prepare yourself for the direction you are heading.

How to Scale

Scaling is more than just about doubling numbers as they relate to marketing, sales, staff, and space. As you grow, you most often need to transition some components of your business to be more streamlined and, perhaps, even automated. You may also need to add new employees who are experienced with larger companies and can provide that solid infrastructure you will need as your company expands.

What works when you are a smaller business doesn't always work when you have grown, and you often have to redevelop your processes to build them for the next stage of your business.

For instance, rather than hiring yet another person, you could integrate the software so the data transfers seamlessly, which can save you a part-time employee. From ordering supplies and managing the billings, to the marketing techniques you start using, there are a variety of ways to streamline and scale your business without having to double payroll.

Your Money Mindset and Raising Your Financial Set Points

We all have our own beliefs about money, and there are many great books written on the subject. It's essential to recognize that some of your own beliefs can hold you back from building a thriving, profitable business.

Do you get uncomfortable talking about money? Do you get uncomfortable asking a client for money during the initial sale? Do you get uncomfortable asking a client to pay when they haven't paid? Do you get uncomfortable sharing with others that you are making more money? If you answered yes, these are all indications that you need to work on your money mindset.

If this is you, make a plan to work on improving your money mindset through a variety of tools such as reading books, listening to podcasts, attending seminars, and working with a coach.

We all have a financial set point that can limit our growth when we start to hit higher revenues. It is important to be aware of the barriers created by your subconscious that will try to keep you safe in your old comfort zone. In *The Big Leap* by Gay Hendricks, Hendricks addresses the upper limit problems we face when our successes can swell to the point where we self-sabotage our growth. Hendricks outlined that if you can identify and remove the fear and false beliefs, you can achieve your true potential and move toward your zone of genius.

When it comes to your money mindset, you must be vigilant to continue to grow your own awareness and protect from backsliding under the pressures of self-doubt.

Building up Your Team so They Don't Sabotage You

If you intend to grow and you grow fast, keep in mind that it's not just your mindset that will need to be addressed. Your team is familiar with the comfortable pace they have enjoyed, and they could ultimately sabotage your business if you don't address it and be ready for it.

As a business grows, often the owner, who is the keeper of the plan, has seen the growth coming for quite some time. This acclimates the subconscious to be ready for the larger payroll, the more significant marketing spends and the bigger cash crunches. All too often, however, the bookkeeper or office manager is in the dark and not privy to all the plans, so when things happen it can be rather fresh, without warning, and rather scary.

Tales from the Trenches

In my case, it all came to a head when the business had more than doubled, but a payment from a client was late coming in. The bookkeeper came for our weekly meeting, and I noticed she was trembling when she handed me some financial reports. I inquired what was wrong and learned that she had been up all night worried about the financials since we usually had a much larger cash cushion to cover growing expenses. I had to sit her down and let her know that it was for me to worry and stress and that if she was concerned, she needed to talk to me, not internalize it and fret.

In later years, as I coached hundreds of business owners, I saw this come up over and over again when businesses doubled, tripled, and even quadrupled. Bookkeepers, who were great at a certain level of revenue, would panic when the numbers grew so fast. Unfortunately, they often share the panic with other team members and the whole event snowballs. Don't let a complete meltdown happen; talk to your bookkeeper early and often about the growth of the firm and to instruct them to come to talk with you if there is a concern. Otherwise, it can cause massive chaos.

And always be aware that the people who worked close with you to get your company to its current maturity and success may in fact not be the right people to help you take the business to its next logical level. If you sense that, part of your money mindset must include evolving your workforce to support the company's profitable growth. You may have to replace people and that can only happen if you have another position to move such a person to or a plan to terminate them.

Growth and Who You Surround Yourself with

As you continue to grow your business, be intentional with who you talk to and what you listen to. Many individuals who mean well will try to talk you out of your growth plans when you move outside of their comfort level.

Surround yourself with other great entrepreneurs who understand growth. They will help you see a bigger world. Most entrepreneurs can only see to the edge of the horizon as they know it. On the other hand, successful entrepreneurs who have grown to double the size of their business can see further out over the horizon and, as a result, can help prepare you for what is to come and can help you uplevel your own horizons.

Growing a business is an incredible journey, especially with a clear plan and a heads up on the potential pitfalls.

Chapter 16 Recap:

- If you plan to grow, start preparing for the day when you are not calling all the shots
- Start early with mapping your long-term plans
- Consider ways to scale your business
- Keep a check on your money mindset, as well as your team's mindset
- Surround yourself with great people who have gone through what you are going through now

Your Action Plan:

1. *Build out your long-term plan and scalability factors*
2. *Raise your financial set point*
3. *Grow your team's financial awareness*

Conclusion

Kristen S. David

Chapter 17: Learning to Stay Focused

Balance is a precarious thing, as we tend to justify why we do or do not stay on task toward our goals. We know what we need to do but staying the course can be difficult when other pressers present on our plate.

Most people have difficulty maintaining the drive to focus their energies on the things that truly matter as the small day-to-day operations continue to infiltrate and sometimes dominate their day.

I know first-hand the reward of getting to the other side. Having a fantastic team manage the systems and the workflows and perform at peak performance is incredible, but it takes work to get there.

It starts with learning to stay focused on what matters.

When an owner has the time to work on the business, it opens up so many more opportunities from building the business and helping more people, to enjoying life and thriving.

It makes me so sad to see business owners continue to work so hard day-after-day in the same hamster wheel when I know if they have someone hold them accountable, they could propel their business to the next level.

Each business has different problems at different times. You must create a plan that tackles what is more important in your situation. For many, this is sales and marketing; for others, it is staffing, and for others, yet it is the financial controls.

What is often difficult for business owners is that when you are on the inside of the box, it is hard to read the instructions on the outside of the box. Have you ever noticed how easy it is to give other business owners advice? That's because it is so evident when you are on the outside looking in. Unfortunately, you are always on the inside, and it is hard to gain the right perspective to see everything clearly as you are emotionally invested in your own business.

Story Time

As I was growing my law firm, there were many bumps and hurdles that caused me to question whether I wanted to continue. One particular day I almost threw in the towel. I came into the office early, the day after tax payments were due. I had mentioned to my team that I had dropped a personal letter with my quarterly tax payment in the outgoing mail basket and that I needed to make sure it was postmarked that day. The next morning, I saw the letter was still in the basket. I was immediately livid as our written policies and procedures had specific provisions for this task. I then went to my desk and found two pleadings that had not been sent out as I had requested the day before. As I turned on my computer, I found two additional things that had not been handled. By this point I was furious. At that moment, I felt that nothing was working. I was seriously ready to hand over the keys to my business to the next human to walk through the door. In my rage, I called my coach to vent that "nothing was going right." He advised me to grab my purse and my keys, lock up and leave the office for a few days. He could tell that I was toxic, and had I remained I may not have had any of my thirteen staff left by the end of the day.

What I needed was to get out of the day to day and gain a new perspective. I spent a day cooling down and then got back on the phone with my coach. He reminded me to stay focused on what matters. I spent the next day mapping out the core elements to get me to my goals, and when I returned to the office, I was recharged and ready to focus on my goals. I was also able to diplomatically address the failures in the systems and course correct so it didn't happen again.

Bottom line, for business owners, the challenge is to identify and focus on what will propel your business forward. Don't get caught up in the weeds. Stay vigilant and get help from a coach or trusted resource, as this is the key ingredient to staying focused and executing the right things to get you to where you want to go.

Kristen S. David

Chapter 18: Putting It All Together

I wrote this book to help busy business owners have a framework for success. The four pillars of successful business management give structure so you can learn to juggle the constant pressures, but this book is also about building systems to give you your freedom.

First, it is crucial to build a plan, taking into consideration both the short-term needs and your long-term goals. Having a routine for re-assessing these needs is imperative to staying on track.

Next, get clear on your ideal audience and building a marketing plan to bring a steady stream of the right clients or customers. This allows you to generate more revenue and increase your profit, so you have more options. The key to this is also systematizing the marketing, so you don't have to do it all yourself.

The most prominent pillar is handling the day-to-day operations, the people, and your office. This is where those critical policies and procedures and systems come together. Having a system for finding and vetting great people makes all the difference. Having a process for servicing your clients or customers is crucial in allowing your team to handle the day-to-day affairs.

By understanding the proper balance to the expenses allows you to pay yourself and have additional profit at the end of the day. Being a good money manager is about reviewing your reports and making decisions. Without sound financial systems, it's hard to manage reports that you can't see.

My wish for each reader is that you continue the journey and find someone who will hold you accountable to your goals so you can break through the hurdles that hold so many down in business and in life.

Cheers to building thriving, successful business!

Acknowledgments

A thank you to the hundreds and hundreds of entrepreneurs I have worked with and from whom I have learned so much. Your stories, your experiences, and your passion for helping people is what has helped make you successful and I am honored to have been a part of your path.

To Don Bowerman, for putting me to work that first Sunday afternoon when I came in for a job interview and for being the greatest mentor and friend. You taught me work-life balance before it was a buzz word and I will always remember your tennis mornings and winter ski mornings that kept you on the top of your game.

To RJon Robins, thank you for seeing in me what I didn't yet see in myself. Had you not given me the opportunity to help lawyers start their law firms, I may never have travelled down this path. Who knew I would so love helping entrepreneurs learn to run their business like a business!

To Robert, thank you for the endless conversations and support, helping me focus and hone my stories.

To my editors, Madeline, CJ, Robert, and Rochelle thank you for your insights and your detailed review.

To my family and friends, thank you for your support and for being on this journey with me.

"I empower entrepreneurs to rise to the challenges of business ownership
so they can thrive with confidence, security and happiness."

Kristen S. David

– Kristen S. David

About the Author

Kristen David, a former trial lawyer who went from working eighty-five hours a week and being a slave to her law firm, built her business up to a million-dollar-plus business that thrived without her. Since selling her business, she now empowers business owners to build profitable businesses that are self-managed.

Born and raised in Southern Oregon, Kristen grew up on a farm where her mother owned and operated Siskiyou Vineyards Winery in Cave Junction. Kristen graduated as valedictorian and went on to attend Lewis & Clark College and Northwestern School of Law. Kristen defended lawyers and doctors in malpractice cases in Portland, Oregon for fifteen years, where she was a partner of a successful law firm before selling her interests.

Kristen's no-nonsense approach and results-oriented methodology has allowed her to help more than 1,500 business owners better manage their businesses. Kristen walks the walk by running her own thriving, profitable business, Upleveling Your Business, virtually while traveling the world. She is dedicated to helping business owners build a business so they can live life freely and "thrive in the moment."

She is an avid fly fisherwoman, geocacher knitter, and she loves to paint small watercolors while traveling. When home, she can often be found in the kitchen, enjoying a glass of wine while cooking wonderful meals. She splits her time between Paris, France, the Pacific Northwest in the United States and traveling.

Website: www.UplevelingYourBusiness.com

Kristen S. David

Email: Kristen@UplevelingYourBusiness.com

Facebook: www.facebook.com/The.Kristen.David

Instagram: www.instagram.com/TheKristenDavid

LinkedIn: www.linkedin.com/in/kristendavid

Thank You

I want to thank you the reader for taking steps to uplevel your business. As a special gift for getting started living the life you are meant to live, go to www.uplevelingyourbusiness.com/free-resources to get a free entrepreneur's tool kit filled with templates, worksheets, and exercises related to the 4 Pillars of Successful Business Management.

I love hearing stories from business owners from all levels. I welcome your emails with comments on the book, the stories I have shared and hopefully you will share a few of your stories and successes with me!

Cheers to upleveling your business and upleveling your life!

Kristen David

Kristen S. David